Ladybird
Dictionary

D1332300

LADYBIRD BOOKS

UK | USA | Canada | Ireland | Australia
India | New Zealand | South Africa

Ladybird Books is part of the Penguin Random House group of companies
whose addresses can be found at global.penguinrandomhouse.com.
www.penguin.co.uk   www.puffin.co.uk   www.ladybird.co.uk

Penguin
Random House
UK

First published 2018
001

Written by Penny Hands, Liz Walter and Kate Woodford
Text copyright © Ladybird Books Ltd, 2018

Illustrations © Ladybird Books Ltd, 2018

Printed in China

A CIP catalogue record for this book is available from the British Library

ISBN: 978–0–241–33610–6

All correspondence to:
Ladybird Books
Penguin Random House Children's
80 Strand, London WC2R 0RL

Contents

A Guide to the *Ladybird Dictionary*

Welcome to the *Ladybird Dictionary*! Here are some useful tips to help you use it.

- When you read a word in a book that you don't understand, you can look it up and find its meaning.
- You can also use the dictionary to check your spelling of a word.

To look up a word, you will need to:

- Find **the letter it begins with**, such as *a* for *animal*.
- Using the **alphabet line** at the side of each page, find the section of the dictionary that lists words beginning with that letter.
- Once you have found that section, use the **guide words** at the top of the page to check if you are on the correct page.
- Look at the **second and third letters** in your word. Do they come between the second and third letters of the alphabet in the two guide words at the top? If they do, you are probably on the correct page. Look down the page until you find your word.

In this dictionary, as well as the meaning of a word, you will find:

- **The part of speech**
- **The different verb forms**
- **The plural form**
- **Examples**: there are lots of examples showing how a word is used in a sentence. The examples can help you:
  - To understand the meaning of the word (for example, *A cube has six sides.*).
  - By showing you words that often come before or after the word you've looked up (for example, *afraid of spiders*, or *go to school*).
  - To understand grammar. For example, they show you if a word is usually used in the negative (*Don't worry!*) or in the past form (*Sara was ill yesterday.*).
- **Useful words**: at the end of the dictionary, there is a section of labelled pictures arranged by subject – these are useful if you are reading or writing about a particular topic.
- **Pictures**: it's much easier to understand a word's meaning if you can see a picture of it – this dictionary has lots of them!

Using the dictionary

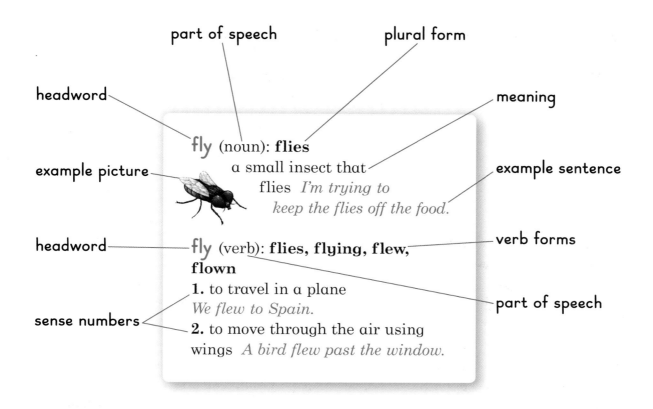

part of speech

plural form

headword

meaning

fly (noun): **flies**

example picture

a small insect that
flies *I'm trying to
keep the flies off the food.*

example sentence

headword

fly (verb): **flies, flying, flew,
flown**

verb forms

1. to travel in a plane
We flew to Spain.

part of speech

sense numbers

2. to move through the air using
wings *A bird flew past the window.*

The **headword** is the first word you come to when you look up a word in the dictionary.

The **part of speech** is the grammar of a word. For example, whether it is a noun, a verb, an adjective, an adverb, or a preposition.

The **plural form** is the way you spell a noun when you are talking about more than one thing. We usually just add *-s* to make a plural, but sometimes we add *-es* or *-ies*.

The **verb forms** are the way a verb changes depending on whether you are talking in the present or the past, or the way you spell the verb when you add *-ing* to it.

The **sense numbers** show you that a word has more than one meaning.

Example sentences show you how a word is typically used in a sentence.

Example pictures help you to understand the meaning of the word by showing you what something looks like.

Aa

above (preposition, adverb)
higher than something
They live in the apartment above us.

across (preposition)
If you go across a place, you go from one side of that place to the other.
A dog was walking across the road.

actor (noun)
a person in a film or a play
He's a famous actor.

actually (adverb)
If you actually do something, you really do it. *I saw her but I didn't actually speak to her.*

add (verb): **adds, adding, added**
1. to put one number with another number and get a new amount
If you add twelve and six you get eighteen.

$$12 + 6 = 18$$

2. to put one thing with another thing *Add a spoon of sugar to the mixture.*

address (noun): **addresses**
information about where you live, for example your house number and street name
Write your name and address here.

admit (verb): **admits, admitting, admitted** to say that you did something bad *Sam admitted to stealing the bike.*

adult (noun)
a person who is older than a child *The tickets are more expensive for an adult than for a child.*

adventure (noun)
something that you do that is exciting and dangerous *Read all about their adventures at sea!*

advice (noun)
something that someone says you should do because it will help you
They give advice about healthy eating.

affect (verb): **affects, affecting, affected** to cause difficulties for someone or something *The party was inside so the rain didn't affect us.*

afford (verb): **affords, affording, afforded** to have enough money to pay for something *I can't afford a new bike.*

afraid (adjective)
feeling that something or someone might hurt you *I'm really afraid of spiders.*

after (preposition)
when something has finished *I play football after school.*

afternoon (noun)
the part of the day after lunch and before the evening *What are you doing this afternoon?*

again (adverb)
1. another time *Could you say that again, please?*
2. like before *I woke for a while but went to sleep again.*

age (noun)
how many years a person has lived *Children start school at the age of seven.*

ago (adverb)
in the past *They arrived here three years ago.*

agree (verb): **agrees, agreeing, agreed**
1. to think the same about something *I agree with Tom that chocolate ice cream is the best.*
2. to say yes to something *If Mum agrees, I will sleep at your house.*

aim (verb): **aims, aiming, aimed**
to try to do a particular thing *I aim to finish the project this week.*

air (noun)
the gases around us that we breathe but cannot see *It was nice to breathe fresh air again.*

airport (noun)
a place where you get on and off a plane *We met them at the airport.*

alien (noun)
a creature from a planet that is not Earth *aliens from outer space*

all right (adjective, adverb)
1. quite good but not very good *The food was all right, but not great.*
2. not hurt or not ill *Are you all right?*

allow (verb): **allows, allowing, allowed** to say that something can happen *Are you allowed to drink water in class?*

along (preposition, adverb)
moving forwards on a road or path *We walked along the path and talked.*

a
b
c
d
e
f
g
h
i
j
k
l
m
n
o
p
q
r
s
t
u
v
w
x
y
z

a
b
c
d
e
f
g
h
i
j
k
l
m
n
o
p
q
r
s
t
u
v
w
x
y
z

alphabet (noun)
all the letters in a language, written one after another
"L"comes after "K" in the alphabet.

already (adverb)
before now *I've already had lunch.*

also (adverb)
as well *I play football and I also play tennis.*

although (conjunction)
but *I like chocolate, although I don't often eat it.*

always (adverb)
1. every time *I always see Lucy in the park.*
2. for all the time that will come *We will always be friends.*

a.m. (abbreviation)
in the morning *9.30 a.m.*

ambulance (noun)
a van for taking people to hospital because they are hurt or ill *Quick, call an ambulance!*

angry (adjective)
not happy with someone because they have done something bad to you *I was angry with her because she lost my phone.*

animal (noun)
a living thing that is not a person or plant *I love all animals, especially cats.*

ankle (noun)
the bottom of your leg, just above your foot *Lara broke her ankle.*

another (pronoun, determiner)
one more *Can I have another cake, please?*

answer (noun)
something you say when someone asks you a question *What was her answer?*

answer (verb): **answers, answering, answered** to say something when someone asks you a question *I asked her how old she was, but she didn't answer.*

apartment (noun)
a home that is on one floor of a big building *They live in a big apartment.*

appear (verb): **appears, appearing, appeared**
1. If someone or something appears, they start to be seen. *Suddenly, a man appeared at the door.*
2. If you appear happy, calm, etc., you look happy, calm, etc. *She appeared perfectly happy.*

apple (noun)
a hard, round fruit, which is green or red on the outside and white inside *apple pie*

area (noun)
a part of a place *There's a play area in the park.*

argue (verb): **argues, arguing, argued** to say angry things to someone because you don't agree with them *Sara and Sophia, stop arguing!*

argument (noun)
when you say angry things to someone because you don't agree with them *Lucas and Samuel had an argument over who was better at football.*

arm (noun)
the long part of your body with a hand on the end *He put his arm around her.*

armchair (noun)
a comfortable chair with parts where you put your arms *Grandad was sitting in his armchair, reading the paper.*

army (noun): **armies**
a large group of people who fight wars for their country *My uncle is in the army.*

around (preposition)
1. on every side of something *There were sheep all around us.*
2. in the opposite direction *I called her name and she turned around.*
3. in the direction of a circle *We walked around the park.*
4. close to a number but not exactly that number *There were around thirty people at the party.*
5. near *Is there a park around here?*

arrive (verb): **arrives, arriving, arrived** to get to somewhere *We arrived in London on Saturday.*

a
b
c
d
e
f
g
h
i
j
k
l
m
n
o
p
q
r
s
t
u
v
w
x
y
z

a b c d e f g h i j k l m n o p q r s t u v w x y z

art (noun)
1. paintings, drawings and other beautiful things that people make with their hands
We visited an art gallery.
2. the activity of painting, drawing and making beautiful things with your hands
We do art on a Wednesday afternoon.

artist (noun)
someone who paints, draws pictures or makes other beautiful things with their hands *Picasso is a famous artist.*

ask (verb): **asks, asking, asked**
to say a question to someone
I asked her how old she was.

asleep (adjective)
sleeping *Is she asleep?*

astronaut (noun)
a person who goes into space and works there
I want to be an astronaut when I grow up.

athlete (noun)
someone who is good at running races, jumping or throwing things
At school, he was a really good athlete.

attack (verb): **attacks, attacking, attacked** to try to hurt someone using hands, or a gun or bomb, etc.
They attacked the enemy.

audience (noun)
the group of people watching a film, play or concert *The audience clapped loudly.*

aunt (noun)
your mother or father's sister, or your uncle's wife *My aunt and uncle came to see us.*

autumn (noun)
the season before winter when trees turn red and yellow *autumn leaves*

awake (adjective)
not sleeping *Is Diego awake yet?*

away (adverb)
1. to a place that is not here
Go away!
2. visiting a different place and not at home *We're away next week.*
3. in the future *My holiday is only a week away!*

awful (adjective)
very bad *I've had an awful day.*

Bb

baby (noun): **babies**
1. a very young child who is under one year old *Isabella has a baby brother.*
2. a very young animal *a baby elephant*

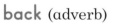

back (adverb)
1. to the direction that is behind *She looked back and waved at us.*
2. returning *I put the book back on the shelf.*

back (noun)
1. the part that is the biggest distance from the front *I usually sit in the back of the car.*
2. the wide part of your body from your neck to your bottom *I had my bag on my back.*

backpack (noun)
a big bag for carrying things on your back *I'm taking a backpack with me.*

backward, backwards (adverb)
to the direction that is behind *Take three steps backwards.*

bad (adjective)
not good *The weather was really bad.*

badminton (noun)
a sport in which you hit a light object over a net using a racket *She plays badminton.*

bag (noun)
a container that you carry things in *He was carrying a bag of shopping.*

ball (noun)
a round object that you use for playing sports *Throw the ball to Amy.*

balloon (noun)
a round object filled with air that is very light and floats *His little sister was holding a balloon.*

banana (noun)
a long, yellow fruit *I ate a banana.*

band (noun)
a group of people who play music together *What's your favourite band?*

bank (noun)
a place that keeps your money safe and also lets you borrow money *I have lots of money in the bank.*

a
b
c
d
e
f
g
h
i
j
k
l
m
n
o
p
q
r
s
t
u
v
w
x
y
z

baseball (noun)
a sport in which you hit a ball with a bat and then run around a square *He plays baseball.*

basketball (noun)
a sport in which you throw a big ball through a round net *Do you play basketball?*

bat (noun)

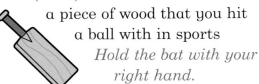

a piece of wood that you hit a ball with in sports *Hold the bat with your right hand.*

bath (noun)
1. a thing that you fill with water and sit in to wash yourself *Olivia is in the bath.*
2. when you sit in a bath that has water in it *I'm going to have a bath.*

bathroom (noun)
1. a room with a bath in it *Daniel is in the bathroom.*
2. the American word for "toilet" *Can I use your bathroom?*

beach (noun): **beaches**
a place next to the sea, which is covered in sand *We spent a day at the beach.*

bean (noun)
a small, round part of a plant which we eat *Lots of the dishes have beans in them.*

bear (noun)
a large, wild animal with fur
a big brown bear

beard (noun)
hair on the bottom part of a man's face *My dad has a beard.*

beat (verb): **beats, beating, beat, beaten** to win against someone in a sport or other competition *We beat them 4–0.*

beautiful (adjective)
very nice to look at *The sky is beautiful this evening.*

because (conjunction)
used for saying why something happens *I was running to school because I was late.*

become (verb): **becomes, becoming, became, become** to start to be something *She became queen at the age of 25.*

bed (noun)
a piece of furniture for sleeping on *Sophie is still in her bed.*

bedroom (noun)
a room where you sleep
That's David's bedroom.

before (preposition, conjunction, adverb) earlier than something
Jacob got to the party before me.

begin (verb): **begins, beginning, began, begun** to start
It began to rain.

behind (preposition)
at the back of *The paper is in the cupboard behind you.*

believe (verb): **believes, believing, believed** to think that something is true *Lucas says he's read all six books but I don't believe him.*

belong (verb): **belongs, belonging, belonged** If something belongs to you, it is yours. *That bag belongs to Gemma.*

below (preposition)
under *They live in the apartment below us.*

belt (noun)
a long piece of leather for wearing around the middle of your body *I need a belt to hold up my trousers.*

best (adjective)
better than all others *Ethan is my best friend.*

best (adverb)
more than any other *I liked the strawberry ice cream best.*

better (adjective)
more successful, useful or interesting *My spelling is getting better.*

better (adverb)
in a way that is more successful *I did better in my maths test this week.*

between (preposition)
1. in the space after one thing and before another thing *Rosie's house is between here and school.*
2. after one time and before another time *I have free time between classes.*

bicycle (noun)
a machine with two wheels that takes you to places when you push parts with your feet *She rides a bicycle to school.*

big (adjective)
large *It's a very big school.*

bike (noun)
a bicycle *Do you ride a bike?*

bin (noun)
a container for rubbish *My pen broke, so I threw it in the bin.*

bird (noun)
a small animal that flies and has a hard, pointed mouth *A bird flew past me.*

birthday (noun)
the date every year on which a person was born *Happy birthday, Johnny!*

biscuit (noun)
a flat, hard food that is usually sweet *She opened a packet of biscuits.*

bit (noun)
a small piece of something *Would you like a bit of chocolate?*

bite (verb): **bites, biting, bit, bitten** to cut something with your teeth *I bit into my sandwich.*

black (adjective)
the darkest colour of night *She has black hair.*

blame (verb): **blames, blaming, blamed** to say that someone has done something bad *Jack blamed me for losing the money.*

blanket (noun)
a cover for a bed, made of a thick, soft material *I was cold so I put an extra blanket on the bed.*

blind (adjective)
If someone is blind, they cannot see. *She was born blind.*

blonde (adjective)
Blonde hair is light yellow. *Klara has blonde hair and blue eyes.*

blood (noun)
the red liquid in your body

blow (verb): **blows, blowing, blew, blown** If the wind blows, it moves. *A strong wind was blowing.*

blue (adjective)
the colour of the sky when the weather is sunny *Heidi has blue eyes.*

board (noun)
a flat piece of wood *There was a board over the broken window.*

boat (noun)
a thing that we use for travelling on water *We took the boat across the lake.*

body (noun): **bodies**
all of a person or animal, including arms, legs and every part *the human body*

bone (noun)
one of the very strong, white parts inside the body *She broke a bone in her arm.*

book (noun)
a set of pages with printed writing on them *I'm reading a good book at the moment.*

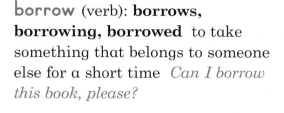

book (verb): **books, booking, booked** to plan to do something by buying a ticket or visiting a website, for example *My mum has booked train tickets.*

bored (adjective)
not interested *There was nothing to do so I was bored.*

boring (adjective)
not interesting *It's a really boring book.*

born: be born (verb)
When a baby is born, they come out of their mother's body. *She was born in March.*

borrow (verb): **borrows, borrowing, borrowed** to take something that belongs to someone else for a short time *Can I borrow this book, please?*

both (determiner, pronoun)
used for saying the same thing about two people or things *Both of us play the piano.*

bottle (noun)
a plastic or glass thing for keeping water, milk, etc., in *a bottle of water*

bottom (noun)
the lowest part of something *These fish live at the bottom of the ocean.*

bowl (noun)
a deep dish for holding food *He gave me a bowl of soup.*

box (noun): **boxes**
a container for keeping things in *We put the books in a cardboard box.*

boy (noun)
a male child *There are fifteen boys in my class.*

bracelet (noun)
a piece of jewellery that you wear on your arm *She was wearing a pretty bracelet.*

a
b
c
d
e
f
g
h
i
j
k
l
m
n
o
p
q
r
s
t
u
v
w
x
y
z

a
b
c
d
e
f
g
h
i
j
k
l
m
n
o
p
q
r
s
t
u
v
w
x
y
z

brave (adjective)
not afraid of things that make most people afraid *I'm not brave enough to jump out of a plane.*

bread (noun)
a food made of flour and water which is baked
I bought a loaf of bread.

break (noun)
when you stop working for a short time *Let's have a break from work.*

break (verb): **breaks, breaking, broke, broken**
1. to divide into two or more parts, often by accident
The plate fell on the floor and broke.
2. If a machine breaks, it stops working. *You've broken my camera!*

breakfast (noun)
the meal that you eat in the morning
Have you had breakfast?

breathe (verb): **breathes, breathing, breathed** to take air in through your mouth or nose and out again *The doctor said, "Breathe in, now breathe out."*

bridge (noun)
something built over a river so that cars and people can go across it
They drove across the bridge.

bright (adjective)
If a colour is bright, it is strong and also light. *Isabel was wearing a bright green dress.*

bring (verb): **brings, bringing, brought** to take something with you
Bring your trainers with you.

broken (adjective)
1. divided into pieces, by accident
broken glass
2. not working *I think this TV is broken.*

brother (noun)
a boy or man who has the same mother and father as you *I have a brother and a sister.*

brown (adjective)
the colour of chocolate or mud
My brother has brown eyes.

brush (noun): **brushes**
an object with a handle and lots of short, stiff pieces, used for painting, cleaning or making your hair tidy
She was painting with a very large brush.

build (verb): **builds, building, built**
to make something by putting parts
together *They are building a house.*

bus (noun): **buses**
a machine that you travel on which
is long and has a lot of seats
Shall we catch the bus into town?

busy (adjective)
doing a lot of things *Daniel is busy
making dinner.*

but (conjunction)
used to join two ideas or facts that
are different *Jack is clever, but he
never does any work.*

butter (noun)
a soft, yellow food that is often
put on bread *bread and butter*

buy (verb): **buys, buying, bought**
to get something from a shop by
giving money for it *Could you buy
some bread, please?*

bye, bye-bye (exclamation)
something you say when you leave
someone *Bye! See you later!*

Cc

café (noun)
a place where you can have drinks
and small meals *We had lunch in
a café.*

cake (noun)
a sweet food
that you make
by mixing together
sugar, butter, eggs
and flour and then
baking them
Would you like a slice of cake?

call (noun)
when you use the telephone
Give me a call this evening.

call (verb): **calls, calling, called**
1. to give a baby a name
They've called him Santiago.
2. to shout *Did you call my name?*
3. to telephone someone *I'll call
you later.*

camel (noun)
a large animal that lives in hot
places and has one or two large,
round parts on its back

camera (noun)
a thing that takes pictures *I used the camera on my mobile phone.*

can (noun)
a metal container for drinks and food *a can of cola*

can (verb)
1. If you can do something, you are able to do it. *Sophie can run really fast.*
2. If you can do something, you are allowed to do it. *Can we go outside?*
3. used to ask someone to do something. *Can you help me, please?*

candy (noun): **candies**
the American word for "sweet"
Would you like a candy?

car (noun)
a machine for travelling on roads that takes four to six people
We could go there by car.

card (noun)
a piece of strong paper that is folded with a picture on the front and a message inside
I got lots of birthday cards.

care (verb): **cares, caring, cared**
to think that someone or something is important *I don't care if she's upset!*

care for (verb): **cares for, caring for, cared for** to give a child or ill person what they need so they are well and safe *She has to care for her very old mother.*

careful (adjective)
If you are careful when you do something, you try hard not to make mistakes. *Be careful with those scissors!*

carrot (noun)
a long, orange vegetable that grows under the ground *raw carrot*

carry (verb): **carries, carrying, carried** to hold someone or something and take them somewhere
She was carrying a baby.

cartoon (noun)
a funny film or programme with people and animals that are not real
I watched a cartoon on TV.

castle (noun)
a very big, old building for keeping people safe when other people were trying to kill them *We visited a castle.*

cat (noun)
a small animal with fur that people keep as a pet *We have a cat.*

a b c d e f g h i j k l m n o p q r s t u v w x y z

catch (verb): **catches, catching, caught**
1. to take something in your hands that was moving through the air *He threw the ball to me and I caught it.*
2. to get on a train or bus *We're going to catch the 6 o'clock train.*

cave (noun)
a big hole in the ground or in the side of a hill *I went into a really dark cave.*

centimetre (noun)
a unit of measurement equal to 0.01 of a metre *I've grown three centimetres this year!*

centre (noun)
the middle of something *We walked around the town centre.*

century (noun): **centuries**
one hundred years
the twenty-first century

certain (adjective)
sure *Are you certain that you saw her?*

chair (noun)
a piece of furniture for one person to sit on
The children all sit on wooden chairs.

chance (noun)
a time when it is possible to do something *I'll talk to Ben if I get the chance.*

change (verb): **changes, changing, changed** to start to be different *The school has changed since I was there.*

character (noun)
a person in a film or book
He's the main character in the book.

cheap (adjective)
If something is cheap, it costs little money to buy. *That was a very cheap ice cream!*

check (verb): **checks, checking, checked** to look at something to find out if it is right *I checked that Martina's name was on the list.*

cheer (verb): **cheers, cheering, cheered** to shout in a happy way at someone who has done something well *We all cheered as the team came out.*

cheese (noun)
a solid yellow or white food made from milk *We had some bread and cheese.*

chemist (noun)
a shop where you can buy medicines *I got some cough mixture from the chemist.*

a
b
c
d
e
f
g
h
i
j
k
l
m
n
o
p
q
r
s
t
u
v
w
x
y
z

chest (noun)
a large, wooden box for putting things in
a pirate's chest

chicken (noun)
1. a farm bird that we eat and get eggs from *The chickens were running around the farmyard.*
2. the meat from a chicken *I had a chicken sandwich.*

child (noun): **children**
a young person who has not grown into an adult yet *There are thirty children in the class.*

chip (noun)
a long, thin piece of potato cooked in oil
We had fish and chips.

chocolate (noun)
a sweet, brown food that you eat as a treat *I bought a bar of chocolate.*

choose (verb): **chooses, choosing, chose, chosen** to decide to have one thing from a group of things
I chose a strawberry ice cream.

church (noun): **churches**
a building where Christians pray to God *They go to church on Sunday.*

cinema (noun)
a building where you can see films on a big screen *Shall we go to the cinema?*

circle (noun)
a round shape
Cut out a circle.

circus (noun): **circuses**
a show in a big tent where you watch people doing difficult things with their bodies
We went to the circus.

city (noun): **cities**
a big place with lots of houses, shops, offices, roads, etc.
I like living in a big city.

class (noun): **classes**
1. a time when people learn something together *I have a maths class till 4 o'clock.*
2. a group of people who learn something together, with the same teacher *Paolo and I are in the same class.*

classroom (noun)
a room where children have school lessons *My classroom gets very hot in the afternoon.*

clean (adjective)
not dirty *Are your hands clean?*

a
b
c
d
e
f
g
h
i
j
k
l
m
n
o
p
q
r
s
t
u
v
w
x
y
z

clean (verb): **cleans, cleaning, cleaned** to use water and soap, so that something is not dirty *Can you help me clean the kitchen?*

clever (adjective)
If someone is clever, they know a lot and learn things very quickly.
He's a very clever boy.

climb (verb): **climbs, climbing, climbed** to go to the top of something *She climbed the ladder.*

clock (noun)
something that shows you the time *The clock on the wall said half past one.*

close (verb): **closes, closing, closed** to move parts together so that something is not open
Could you close the window, please?

closed (adjective)
If something is closed, parts are together so that it is not open.
The door was closed.

clothes (noun)
things that we cover our bodies with, for example T-shirts, trousers and coats *Wear some warm clothes.*

cloud (noun)
a white or grey thing in the sky that is made of water *Are those rain clouds?*

clown (noun)
a person in funny clothes who makes people laugh by falling over and doing other silly things *a circus clown*

club (noun)
a group of people who often meet so they can do an activity together *Sue is in the chess club at school.*

coat (noun)
a warm piece of clothing for wearing over other clothes *It's cold outside, so put your coat on!*

coconut (noun)
a large, brown nut which is white inside and has liquid in the middle

coffee (noun)
a hot drink made by mixing water with a brown powder made of coffee beans *Would you like a cup of coffee?*

coin (noun)
a round piece of metal with pictures and writing on it, used as money
He had a few coins in his pocket.

cold (adjective, noun)
with a temperature that is low
It's cold outside!

a b c d e f g h i j k l m n o p q r s t u v w x y z

collect (verb): **collects, collecting, collected** to get something from a place *Could you collect your books from the office?*

college (noun)
a place where people study after they have finished going to school *Laura goes to college.*

colour (noun)
red, blue, yellow, etc.
Blue is my favourite colour.

come (verb): **comes, coming, came, come**
1. to go to this place *Come here!*
2. to go somewhere with someone *Come to the park with us.*

comic (noun)
a thin book for children with stories told in pictures *He was reading a comic.*

competition (noun)
something in which people try to do an activity better than other people *I've entered a poetry competition at school.*

complete (verb): **completes, completing, completed**
to finish something by adding the last part *It took six months to complete the building.*

completely (adverb)
very *It's a completely different game.*

computer (noun)
a machine that keeps information and is used for many things, for example getting information from the internet
My mum does all her work on a computer.

control (verb): **controls, controlling, controlled**
to make someone or something do what you want them to *You control the robot with these buttons here.*

conversation (noun)
when you talk with someone *I was having a conversation with George.*

cook (verb): **cooks, cooking, cooked** to prepare food so that you can eat it *My sister was cooking in the kitchen.*

cookie (noun)
the American word for "biscuit"
chocolate-chip cookies

cool (adjective)
1. rather cold
I had a nice cool glass of lemonade.
2. good *Louie had some really cool ideas.*

copy (verb): **copies, copying, copied** to do exactly the same as someone or something else *Don't copy Amy – do your own drawing!*

corner (noun)
the point where two lines or roads join *He was standing on the corner of the street.*

correct (adjective)
right; having no mistakes *That was the correct answer!*

could (verb)
1. used for talking about something that is possible *They could arrive this afternoon.*
2. used for politely asking someone for something or asking them to do something *Could I borrow your pen, please?*
3. the past form of "can" *Our teacher said we could leave.*

country (noun)
1. countries an area of land with its own name and its own government *Russia is the largest country in the world.*
2. land away from the city with lots of grass and trees, etc. *They live in the country.*

countryside (noun)
land away from the city with lots of grass, trees and plants *The countryside is beautiful there.*

cousin (noun)
a child of your uncle or aunt *My cousins are coming to stay.*

cover (verb): **covers, covering, covered** to put something over the top of something else *I covered the food with a cloth.*

cow (noun)
a large animal that farmers keep for its meat and milk *Cows were grazing in the field.*

crazy (adjective)
very strange *He has some crazy ideas!*

create (verb): **creates, creating, created** to make something *She creates these beautiful pictures.*

crocodile (noun)
a long animal with lots of sharp teeth that lives in water

cross (verb): **crosses, crossing, crossed** If you cross a road or river, you go from one side of it to the other. *Find a safe place to cross the road.*

a
b
c
d
e
f
g
h
i
j
k
l
m
n
o
p
q
r
s
t
u
v
w
x
y
z

a
b
c
d
e
f
g
h
i
j
k
l
m
n
o
p
q
r
s
t
u
v
w
x
y
z

crown (noun)
a round, metal thing that a king or queen wears on their head *They tried to steal the queen's crown.*

cruel (adjective)
Someone who is cruel likes doing bad things to other people and making them sad.
He was a horrible, cruel man.

cry (verb): **cries, crying, cried**
When you cry, water comes from your eyes because you are sad.
Please don't cry!

cup (noun)
a thing with an open top that you drink from
Would you like a cup of coffee?

cupboard (noun)
a piece of furniture with shelves inside, where you keep things that you need *He took the plates out of the cupboard.*

curly (adjective)
Curly hair is not straight. *She has lovely curly dark hair.*

cut (verb): **cuts, cutting, cut**
to use a knife or scissors, for example, to make one thing become two or more things *My mum cut the cake into eight pieces.*

Dd

dad, daddy (noun)
a child's word for "father"
Dad, can you help me?

dance (verb): **dances, dancing, danced** to move your body to music
We were dancing to our favourite songs.

danger (noun)
the possibility that you will be hurt or killed *There was a sign by the water that said, "Danger! Keep out!"*

dangerous (adjective)
able to hurt or kill you *These animals are dangerous.*

dark (adjective)
without light, so that you cannot see *It was dark so I put the light on.*

date (noun)
the name and number of a day in the year *The date is the 3rd of March 2019.*

daughter (noun)
your child who is a girl
They have two sons and a daughter.

day (noun)
each 24 hours that we divide the week into *Which day are you leaving? Saturday?*

dead (adjective)
not living *Her grandfather is dead.*

dear (adjective)
used at the start of a letter to someone, before their name
Dear Lara, How are you doing?

death (noun)
the end of life *She was very upset by the death of her grandfather.*

decide (verb): **decides, deciding, decided** to choose to do something
We decided to go to the park.

deep (adjective)
If something is deep, it is a long way from the top to the bottom.
Be careful – the water is deep!

dentist (noun)
someone whose job is to repair teeth *I have a dentist's appointment after school.*

depend: it/that depends (phrase)
used to say that the answer to a question changes when the facts change *I'm not sure when we'll get there. It depends on whether we walk or drive.*

describe (verb): **describes, describing, described** to say facts about something or someone *Describe your best friend.*

desert (noun)
a large, hot area with lots of sand and no water *They crossed the desert on camels.*

desk (noun)
a table that you write or work at *I was sitting at my desk, writing.*

diary (noun): **diaries** a book in which you write about what you have done each day *Do you keep a diary?*

dictionary (noun): **dictionaries** a book with a list of words which tells you what those words mean *I looked the words up in a dictionary.*

die (verb): **dying, dies, died** to stop living *Lisa's cat died at the weekend.*

difference (noun)
something that makes two people or things not the same *What's the difference between these two books?*

a
b
c
d
e
f
g
h
i
j
k
l
m
n
o
p
q
r
s
t
u
v
w
x
y
z

different (adjective)
not the same *Our new house is very different from our old house.*

dining room (noun)
a room in the house where you eat
We had dinner in the dining room.

dinner (noun)
the biggest meal of the day, usually eaten in the evening
What are we having for dinner?

dinosaur (noun)
a big animal that lived a very long time ago *We saw some dinosaur bones at the museum.*

dirty (adjective)
not clean *My hands are dirty.*

disappear (verb): **disappears, disappearing, disappeared**
If someone or something disappears, you suddenly cannot see them.
I was talking to James a moment ago and then he just disappeared!

discover (verb): **discovers, discovering, discovered** to find something or a fact for the first time
We discovered lots of interesting facts about trees.

do (verb)
1. does, doing, did, done
to make an action *I've already done my homework.*
2. does, did
used before another verb to make a question or a negative phrase
Do you like cheese?

doctor (noun)
someone whose job is to help people who are ill or hurt *The doctor gave me some medicine.*

dog (noun)
an animal with fur that is often kept as a pet
Could you take the dog for a walk?

doll (noun)
a child's toy that is like a small person
Molly was playing with her doll.

dolphin (noun)
a clever, grey sea animal with a long nose *The dolphin swam past us.*

don't worry (phrase)
used to tell someone not to be upset about a situation *Don't worry! I can do the shopping.*

door (noun)
the flat part of a building that you open when you enter a room
I opened the door and walked in.

down (adverb)
towards a place that is lower
She fell down the stairs.

downstairs (adverb)
to a lower part of a building
I went downstairs to speak to Mum.

dragon (noun)
in stories, a big creature that breathes fire and has wings and a long tail

draw (verb): **draws, drawing, drew, drawn**
to make a picture using a pencil
Tom drew a picture of his dad.

drawing (noun)
a picture done with a pencil
Maisie did a drawing of her cat.

dress (noun): **dresses**
a piece of clothing often for a woman or girl that covers the main part of their body and part of their legs
Holly was wearing a red dress.

dress up (verb): **dresses up, dressing up, dressed up**
to wear special clothes that make you look like someone else, for example a character from a film *Oliver dressed up as Superman.*

drink (noun)
a liquid that you take into your body through your mouth
I'd love a drink of water.

drink (verb): **drinks, drinking, drank, drunk**
to take a liquid into your body through your mouth
I drank some apple juice.

drive (verb): **drives, driving, drove, driven**
to go somewhere in a car
We drove to the party.

drop (verb): **drops, dropping, dropped** to let something fall to the floor *I dropped the glass that I was holding.*

dry (adjective)
If something is dry, there is no water on it. *The clothes are all dry.*

duck (noun)
a bird with short legs that lives near water
We went to feed the ducks.

during (preposition)
If something happens during a period of time, it happens in that period. *We usually go on holiday during the summer.*

a
b
c
d
e
f
g
h
i
j
k
l
m
n
o
p
q
r
s
t
u
v
w
x
y
z

a
b
c
d
e
f
g
h
i
j
k
l
m
n
o
p
q
r
s
t
u
v
w
x
y
z

Ee

each (pronoun, determiner)
every one *Each of the children got a present.*

ear (noun)
one of the two things on the side of your head that you hear with *He whispered something in her ear.*

early (adjective, adverb)
before the time that something starts *We got to the station early.*

Earth (noun)
the planet where we live *Planet Earth*

east (noun)
the direction on the right of a map *They live in the east of the country.*

easy (adjective)
not difficult *Our homework this week is really easy.*

eat (verb): **eats, eating, ate, eaten**
to put food in your body through your mouth *You should always eat breakfast.*

edge (noun)
the part of something that is furthest away from the middle *The house is on the edge of a forest.*

education (noun)
the activity of teaching and learning *He had a very good education.*

egg (noun)
a round thing that a chicken makes, eaten as food *I had a boiled egg for breakfast.*

either (pronoun, determiner, conjunction)
used to say that both people or things are possible and you can choose which you want *"Lemonade or cola?" "Either, thanks."*

elephant (noun)
a very big, grey animal with a very long nose

elevator (noun)
the American word for "lift" *Shall we take the elevator?*

elf (noun): **elves**
in children's stories, a very small person who can do magic

else (adverb)
as well as something
What else did you do?

email (noun)
a message that you send to someone
using a computer *I sent Lara an
email this morning.*

email (verb): **emails, emailing,
emailed** to send a message using a
computer *Have you emailed Tom?*

empty (adjective)
If something is empty, it has nothing
in it. *an empty bottle*

end (noun)
the last part of something *We're just
watching the end of the film.*

end (verb): **ends, ending, ended**
to stop *The game is about to end.*

enemy (noun): **enemies**
someone who hates you and wants to
do bad things to you *He didn't have
any enemies.*

English (noun)
the language that people speak in
the UK, USA and other parts of the
world *Do you speak English?*

enjoy (verb): **enjoys, enjoying,
enjoyed** to like doing something
The boys enjoy drawing and painting.

enormous (adjective)
very big *Their garden is enormous.*

enough (adjective, pronoun, adverb)
as much or as many as you need *We
don't have enough time to walk there.*

enter (verb): **enters, entering,
entered** to go in somewhere.
Enter the building from Green Street.

entrance (noun)
a door where you can go in a
building *Meet me at the main
entrance.*

envelope (noun)
a flat paper
container that
a letter goes in
*I opened
the envelope.*

environment (noun)
nature around us, for example the
sea, trees and plants *We must
protect the environment.*

eraser (noun)
the American word for "rubber"

a
b
c
d
e
f
g
h
i
j
k
l
m
n
o
p
q
r
s
t
u
v
w
x
y
z

a
b
c
d
e
f
g
h
i
j
k
l
m
n
o
p
q
r
s
t
u
v
w
x
y
z

escape (verb): **escapes, escaping, escaped** to leave a place where you do not want to be, often without people knowing *He escaped from prison.*

etc. (abbreviation, adverb) used after a list of words to mean that you could add more to the list *We have a cupboard here for paper, paints, etc.*

evening (noun) the time after afternoon and before the night *We usually watch TV in the evening.*

ever (adverb) at any time *Have you ever been to the USA?*

every (adjective) all of a group of people or things *Every child in the school has their own laptop.*

everybody, everyone (pronoun) all people *Everyone we asked came to the party.*

everything (pronoun) all things *Have you got everything you need?*

everywhere (adverb) all places *I've looked everywhere for that book.*

exam (noun) a test of what you know about a subject *Maria passed her English exam.*

excellent (adjective) very good *The schools here are excellent.*

except (preposition) but not *I like all vegetables except carrots.*

excited (adjective) very happy about something that you are going to do *Eva is very excited about her birthday tomorrow.*

exciting (adjective) If something that is going to happen is exciting, it makes you feel very happy. *We're going on holiday tomorrow – it's very exciting!*

excuse me (phrase) used for politely getting someone to listen to you *Excuse me, could you tell me where Bond Street is, please?*

exercise (noun) when you move your body many times so it becomes strong and healthy *Do you do much exercise?*

expect (verb): **expects, expecting, expected** to think that something will happen *I expect Anna will come too.*

expensive (adjective)
If something is expensive, you must pay a lot of money to buy it. *expensive clothes*

explain (verb): **explains, explaining, explained**
to tell someone the reasons for something so they understand it *I tried to explain the problem.*

explore (verb): **explores, exploring, explored** to visit a place you have not been to before and look around it *I love exploring new places.*

eye (noun)
one of the two parts of the face that you see with *Close your eyes and go to sleep.*

Ff

face (noun)
the part of the head with the eyes, nose and mouth *I could see from her face that she was sad.*

fact (noun)
a piece of information that we know is true *We know he visited the town last year – that is a fact.*

factory (noun): **factories**
a place where lots of things are made using machines *a shoe factory*

fail (verb): **fails, failing, failed**
to not do something good that you were trying to do *She failed her driving test.*

fair (adjective)
1. If you are fair, you give everyone the same chance. *I try to be fair and treat all the children the same.*
2. Fair hair is light yellow. *Sophie has fair hair and blue eyes.*

fairy (noun): **fairies**
in children's stories, a small person with wings who can do magic

a
b
c
d
e
f
g
h
i
j
k
l
m
n
o
p
q
r
s
t
u
v
w
x
y
z

fall (noun)
the American word for "autumn"

fall (verb): **falls, falling, fell, fallen**
to go down to the ground by accident
Jamie fell off his scooter and hurt his knee.

fall over (verb): **falls over, falling over, fell over, fallen over** to go down to the ground by accident
Ben fell over in the playground.

family (noun): **families**
a group of people who are related, especially parents and their children
My family are coming to the concert.

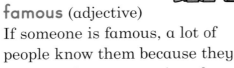

famous (adjective)
If someone is famous, a lot of people know them because they are a good actor or writer, for example. *He's a famous writer.*

fan (noun)
someone who likes a famous person, a type of music or a sports team, for example *football fans*

far (adverb): **farther or further, farthest or furthest** used to say how many kilometres/metres, etc., away something is *How far is it to the nearest swimming pool?*

farm (noun)
a place where plants are grown and animals are kept for food
He owns a dairy farm.

farmer (noun)
someone who owns a farm
a dairy farmer

fashion (noun)
the style of clothes and hair that most people like at a particular time
Fashions are always changing.

fast (adjective)
quick *You're a very fast walker!*

fast (adverb)
quickly *Run as fast as you can.*

fat (adjective)
Someone who is fat is too heavy, usually because they eat too much.
You're not fat!

father (noun)
your parent who is a man
Sylvia's father and mother are both tall.

favourite (adjective)
Your favourite person or thing is the one that you like more than the others. *What's your favourite ice cream?*

fear (noun)
a bad feeling you get when you are in danger *He was shaking with fear.*

feed (verb): **feeds, feeding, fed**
to give food to a person or an animal *Shall we go and feed the lamb?*

feel (verb): **feels, feeling, felt**
1. to have an emotion *I felt so happy.*
2. to touch something with your hand *She felt his cheek and it was hot.*

fetch (verb): **fetches, fetching, fetched** to get something from a different place *Could you fetch a chair from the other room?*

few: a few (determiner, pronoun)
a small number of *We played a few games.*

field (noun)
an area of land where animals are kept or plants are grown for food
There were cows grazing in the field.

fight (noun)
when people try to hurt each other by hitting with their hands and feet *There was a fight in the playground.*

fight (verb): **fights, fighting, fought** to try to hurt someone by hitting them with your hands and feet *Stop fighting, boys!*

film (noun)
a story shown in moving pictures *We went to see a film at the cinema.*

find (verb): **finds, finding, found**
to get something after looking for it *I can't find my scarf.*

find out (verb): **finds out, finding out, found out** to find information *Can you find out when Emily is arriving?*

fine (adjective)
well and not ill *"How are you?" "I'm fine, thanks."*

finger (noun)
one of the five long parts on your hand *She pointed her finger at me.*

finish (verb): **finishes, finishing, finished**
1. to do the last part of something *Have you finished your essay?*
2. to end *The film is about to finish.*

fire (noun)
the hot, orange gas that is made when something burns *The house was on fire.*

fire engine (noun)
a large van for taking firefighters and special equipment to places that are on fire *The fire engines soon arrived.*

firefighter (noun)
a person whose job is to stop fires *Holly's dad is a firefighter.*

first (adjective, adverb, pronoun)
before all other people or things *Dan was the first to arrive.*

fish (noun): **fish or fishes**
an animal that lives in water and swims *There were lots of fish in the pond.*

fit (verb): **fits, fitting, fitted**
If clothes fit, they are the right size for your body. *These shoes don't fit me any more.*

fix (verb): **fixes, fixing, fixed**
to change something that is damaged so that it works again *My bike needs fixing.*

flag (noun)
a piece of cloth with a pattern on it that is a symbol of a country *The Japanese flag is red and white.*

flashlight (noun)
the American word for "torch"

flat (adjective)
smooth, with no raised parts *a flat surface*

flat (noun)
a home that is on one floor of a big building *They live in a flat.*

floor (noun)
1. the lower part inside a building that you walk on *She put her bag down on the floor.*
2. all the rooms in a building that are on the same level *Their office is on the third floor.*

flower (noun)
the beautiful part of a plant that is brightly coloured *We bought my mum a bunch of flowers.*

fly (noun): **flies**
a small insect that flies *I'm trying to keep the flies off the food.*

fly (verb): **flies, flying, flew, flown**
1. to travel in a plane *We flew to Spain.*
2. to move through the air using wings *A bird flew past the window.*

foggy (adjective)
If the weather is foggy, you cannot see well because there are clouds close to the ground. *It was a foggy day.*

follow (verb): **follows, following, followed** to go behind someone in the same direction as them *You know the way so I'll just follow you.*

food (noun)
things that you can eat *If you are hungry, we could have some food.*

foot (noun): **feet**
the part of your body on the end of your leg that you stand on *Sam has such big feet!*

football (noun)
a game in which two teams of eleven players try to kick a ball into a net *They both play football.*

foreign (adjective)
from a different country *I'd like to learn a foreign language.*

forest (noun)
a large area of trees *We went for a walk in the forest.*

forget (verb): **forgets, forgetting, forgot, forgotten** to not remember something *I forgot to post the letter.*

fork (noun)
a thing that you use for eating, with three or four sharp points
a knife and fork

forward, forwards (adverb)
in the direction in front
The car moved forwards again.

free (adjective)
If a person or an animal is free, they are not in prison or a cage.
He was just glad to be free again.

fresh (adjective)
Fresh food has just been grown and has not been frozen or changed to make it last a long time. *fresh fruit and vegetables*

fridge (noun)
a cold cupboard in the kitchen where you keep milk, cheese and other fresh foods *There is some cheese in the fridge.*

friend (noun)
someone that you know and like
Amelia is one of my best friends.

a
b
c
d
e
f
g
h
i
j
k
l
m
n
o
p
q
r
s
t
u
v
w
x
y
z

a
b
c
d
e
f
g
h
i
j
k
l
m
n
o
p
q
r
s
t
u
v
w
x
y
z

friendly (adjective)
If someone is friendly, they are nice and kind to you. *The waiters here are very friendly.*

fries (plural noun)
the American word for "chips" *Do you want fries with your fish?*

frightened (adjective)
feeling that something or someone might hurt you *She's frightened of dogs.*

frog (noun)
a small, green animal that lives partly in water and moves by jumping *There were lots of frogs in the pond.*

front (adjective)
A front door, garden or seat, etc., is at the side of something that points forwards. *Do you want to sit in the front seat?*

front (noun)
the side of something that you usually see because it points forwards *I didn't see the front of the house.*

fruit (noun): **fruit**
apples, bananas, etc., that we eat that grow on trees or bushes *Would you like a piece of fruit?*

full (adjective)
If a container or room is full, it contains as much as it can. *The bottle was full.*

fun (noun)
the feeling of enjoying doing something *Did you have fun at William's house?*

funny (adjective)
Someone or something that is funny makes you laugh. *That's a really funny film.*

future (noun)
the time that will come and has not happened yet *I don't worry about the future.*

Gg

game (noun)
an activity that you do for fun
a game of chess

garden (noun)
an area with plants and grass, near
a house *Let's play in the garden.*

gas (noun): **gases**
a substance like air, used for cooking
and heating *a gas oven*

gate (noun)
a door in a fence
or low wall *Don't
leave the gate open.*

geography (noun)
the study of countries, land, rivers,
mountains, etc.

get (verb): **gets, getting, got**
to obtain or take something
Let's get a sandwich.

get dressed (verb)
to put your clothes on
I got up and got dressed.

get undressed (verb)
to take your clothes off
*She got undressed, ready for
her shower.*

get up (verb): **gets up,
getting up, got up**
to get out of bed
after sleeping *I get
up at 6 o'clock.*

ghost (noun)
the spirit of a dead person that
some people think they can see
*They say there's a ghost in the
old castle.*

gift (noun)
something that someone gives
you; a present
wedding gifts

giraffe (noun)
an African
animal with
a very long neck

girl (noun)
a female child *a baby girl*

give (verb): **gives, giving, gave,
given** to provide something for
someone *I gave him a present.*

glad (adjective)
pleased *I'm glad you could come.*

a
b
c
d
e
f
g
h
i
j
k
l
m
n
o
p
q
r
s
t
u
v
w
x
y
z

glass (noun)
a hard, clear substance, used to make bottles and windows
Ivan collects pennies in a glass jar.

glasses (plural noun)
things you wear in front of your eyes to help you see better *a pair of glasses*

glove (noun)
a soft covering to keep your hand warm *a pair of gloves*

glue (noun)
a sticky substance that sticks things together *We stuck the paper shapes on with glue.*

go (verb): **goes, going, went, gone**
to move from one place to another
I go to school on the bus.

goal (noun)
a point in games like football
She scored three goals.

goat (noun)
an animal that is kept for milk
I don't like goat's milk.

gold (noun)
a yellow metal that is worth a lot of money *a gold ring*

golf (noun)
a sport where you hit small, white balls into holes in the ground
Billy loves playing golf.

good (adjective)
1. high quality; enjoyable
He's a really good teacher.
2. A good person does not do bad things. *She is a good witch.*

goodbye (exclamation)
something you say when you are leaving someone

government (noun)
the people that control a country
The government provides education for everyone.

grade (noun)
a letter or number that tells you how good your work is *She got very good grades in her exams.*

grandchild (noun): **grandchildren**
the son or daughter of your son or daughter

granddaughter (noun)
the daughter of your son or daughter

grandfather (noun)
the father of your mother or father

grandparent (noun)
the mother or father of your mother
or father

grandson (noun)
the son of your son or daughter

grape (noun)
a small, round
red or green fruit
a bunch of grapes

grass (noun)
a plant with thin green leaves
that covers the ground *Don't walk
on the grass.*

great (adjective)
very good *We had a great time.*

green (adjective)
the colour of grass, made by
mixing blue and yellow *She wore
a green dress.*

grey (adjective)
the colour made by mixing black
and white *He has grey hair.*

ground (noun)
the surface of the Earth that you
can stand on *We lay on the
hard ground.*

group (noun)
several things or people in one place
a group of soldiers

grow (verb): **grows, growing,
grew, grown** to get bigger
He's grown a lot this year.

grown-up (noun)
someone that is not a child or
teenager *Is there a grown-up
with you?*

guess (verb): **guesses, guessing,
guessed** to try to give an answer
when you are not sure about
something *Guess how old he is!*

guest (noun)
someone you have invited to your
house *There were over 50 guests at
the party.*

guilty (adjective)
feeling bad because you have done
something wrong *I felt guilty about
making her cry.*

guitar (noun)
a musical instrument with
strings you play with
your fingers
*Anna plays
the guitar
in a band.*

a
b
c
d
e
f
g
h
i
j
k
l
m
n
o
p
q
r
s
t
u
v
w
x
y
z

Hh

hair (noun)
the thin threads that grow on your head *He has short curly hair.*

half (noun, adjective): **halves**
one of two equal parts of something *She gave me half a slice of bread.*

hall (noun)
a long narrow area in a building that leads to other rooms *Leave your shoes in the hall.*

hand (noun)
the part of your body that has fingers *Raise your hand if you know the answer.*

handbag (noun)
a bag that women carry, for small things like keys and a purse *My phone is in my handbag.*

handsome (adjective)
A handsome man has an attractive face. *a handsome prince*

hang (verb): **hangs, hanging, hung** to attach something at the top, with the bottom part free *I hung the washing on the line.*

happen (verb): **happens, happening, happened** to be done; take place *What happened to your face?*

happy (adjective)
in a good mood *I'm happy because we have a day off school.*

hard (adjective)
1. difficult
This homework is very hard.
2. difficult to bend or press
The box is made of hard plastic.

hat (noun)
a piece of clothing you wear on your head *You need to wear a sun hat.*

hate (verb): **hates, hating, hated** to dislike very much *Rory hates cheese.*

have (verb): **has, having, had** to own or possess something *They have a big house.*

head (noun)
the top part of your body, that holds your eyes, mouth, brain, etc. *Louis banged his head on the cupboard door.*

headache (noun)
pain in your head *Danny's got a bad headache.*

headteacher (noun)
the person that is in charge of a school *I had to go to the headteacher's office.*

health (noun)
the condition of your body; whether you are ill or not *My grandfather is 90 but his health is still good.*

healthy (adjective)
not ill *All these fresh vegetables keep us healthy.*

hear (verb): **hears, hearing, heard** to notice sounds with your ears *Did you hear that noise?*

heart (noun)
the part of your body that pumps blood around *My heart was beating very fast.*

heavy (adjective)
weighing a lot *The suitcase was very heavy.*

height (noun)
how high or tall something is *My brother is the same height as me.*

helicopter (noun)
an aircraft with thin parts on top that move round and round *They were rescued by helicopter.*

hello (exclamation)
something you say when you meet someone

help (verb): **helps, helping, helped** to do something to make things easier for someone *Can I help you carry those bags?*

hide (verb): **hides, hiding, hid, hidden** to put something where other people can't find it *I hid the letter inside a book.*

high (adjective)
a long way from the bottom to the top *high mountains*

hill (noun)
a raised area of land *We walked to the top of the hill.*

hippopotamus (noun)
a large animal with thick grey skin that lives in or near water

history (noun)
the study of things that happened in the past

hit (verb): **hits, hitting, hit**
to bang something with your hand
He hit me on the arm.

hobby (noun): **hobbies**
an activity that you do in your spare time *My hobbies are painting and playing video games.*

hockey (noun)
a sport where you try to hit a ball into a net with long wooden sticks

hold (verb): **holds, holding, held**
to have something in your hands
He was holding a large book.

hole (noun)
a space or gap in something
There's a hole in my trousers.

holiday (noun)
a time when you do not work or study and when you might go away somewhere *We went on holiday to France.*

home (adverb)
to the place where you live
It's time to go home.

home (noun)
the place where someone lives
She usually leaves home at 7 a.m.

homework (noun)
work that your teacher gives you to do at home *Have you done your homework?*

honey (noun)
a sweet, sticky food made by bees
bread and honey

hop (verb): **hops, hopping, hopped**
to jump up and down on one leg
She hopped across the room.

hope (verb): **hopes, hoping, hoped**
to want something to happen
I hope we win the competition.

horrible (adjective)
very unpleasant
The food was horrible.

horse (noun)
a large animal that people ride
He was riding a big black horse.

hospital (noun)
a place where doctors and nurses try to make ill people healthy
She was in hospital for four days.

hot (adjective)
with a very high temperature
I felt better after a hot bath.

hotel (noun)
a building where you pay for a room to sleep in *We stayed in a lovely hotel in Paris.*

hour (noun)
a period of sixty minutes
All lessons are an hour long.

house (noun)
a building where people live
Our house has three bedrooms.

how long (phrase)
something you say to ask about the time something takes *How long have you been waiting?*

how many (phrase)
something you say to ask about the number of something *How many people came to the show?*

how much (phrase)
something you say to ask about the amount of something
How much rice would you like?

how often (phrase)
something you say to ask about the number of times that something happens *How often do you tidy your room?*

how old (phrase)
something you say to ask about someone's age *How old is your sister?*

human (noun)
a person *There were no humans on Earth when dinosaurs were alive.*

hundred (noun)
the number 100 *She is nearly a hundred years old.*

hungry (adjective)
feeling that you want to eat something *Lunch is ready. Are you hungry?*

hurry (verb): **hurries, hurrying, hurried** to move quickly or do something quickly *If we don't hurry, we'll miss the train.*

hurt (verb): **hurts, hurting, hurt**
to cause pain or to feel pain
My leg hurts.

husband (noun)
a man that someone is married to
My husband is an engineer.

a
b
c
d
e
f
g
h
i
j
k
l
m
n
o
p
q
r
s
t
u
v
w
x
y
z

a
b
c
d
e
f
g
h
i
j
k
l
m
n
o
p
q
r
s
t
u
v
w
x
y
z

Ii

ice (noun)
frozen water *Don't slip on the ice!*

ice cream (noun)
a soft, sweet food
made from frozen milk
vanilla ice cream

idea (noun)
a thought about something you
can do *I've got a great idea – let's
go to the beach!*

ill (adjective)
not healthy *Grandma was feeling ill.*

imagine (verb): **imagines,
imagining, imagined**
to make a picture in your mind
Imagine you are on a boat.

immediately (adverb)
at once *You must leave immediately.*

important (adjective)
1. Important things affect you a lot.
*It is important to drink plenty
of water.*
2. Important people have a lot of
power. *a very important person*

impossible (adjective)
not possible *Her handwriting is
impossible to read.*

improve (verb): **improves,
improving, improved**
to get better *The weather
has improved.*

include (verb): **includes, including,
included** to have something as part
of a larger thing *The book includes
information about plants.*

increase (verb): **increases,
increasing, increased**
to get bigger *The size of the city
has increased.*

information (noun)
facts about something *I need some
information about train times.*

injury (noun): **injuries**
damage to your body
She had a serious leg injury.

insect (noun)
a small
creature
with six legs,
e.g. a fly or
an ant
*The leaves
were covered
with insects.*

inside (adverb, preposition)
in or into a room or a container
Let's go inside and sit down.

inside (noun)
the part of something that is
under the surface *The inside of
the case is made of plastic.*

instrument (noun)
something such
as a piano or a
violin that you
play to make
music *Sarah
plays several
musical
instruments.*

interesting (adjective)
Interesting things hold your
attention. *This is a really
interesting museum.*

internet (noun)
a system for sharing information
between computers all over the
world *I've seen pictures of eagles
on the internet.*

into (preposition)
from the outside to the inside
of something *They went into
the building.*

introduce (verb): **introduces,
introducing, introduced**
to tell someone another person's
name when they meet for the
first time *Amy introduced me
to her friend.*

invite (verb): **invites, inviting,
invited** to ask someone to do
something such as come to your
house or go to a party with you
*They invited us to stay for
the weekend.*

island (noun)
an area of
land with
water all
around it
*We stayed
on an island
in the middle
of the sea.*

a
b
c
d
e
f
g
h
i
j
k
l
m
n
o
p
q
r
s
t
u
v
w
x
y
z

Jj

a
b
c
d
e
f
g
h
i
j
k
l
m
n
o
p
q
r
s
t
u
v
w
x
y
z

jacket (noun)
a short coat
*The men must
wear jackets and ties.*

jam (noun)
a food made of fruit and sugar that
you eat on bread *strawberry jam*

jeans (plural noun)
trousers made from
strong blue cloth
*We aren't allowed
to wear jeans
to school.*

job (noun)
the work you do to earn money
Mum's got a new job at the hospital.

join (verb): **joins, joining, joined**
to become a member *I joined the
running club last year.*

joke (noun)
something that you say to make
people laugh *She told some really
funny jokes.*

journey (noun)
when you travel from one place to
another *The journey to Alaska took
over a week.*

judge (noun)
a person who is in charge of a court
and decides what punishment a
criminal should get *The judge sent
her to prison for three years.*

juice (noun)
liquid that
comes from fruit
or vegetables
orange juice

jump (verb): **jumps, jumping,
jumped**
to push your body off the ground
with your legs *The boy jumped
over the fence.*

jungle (noun)
an area of
land in a
hot wet
country,
where
plants and
trees grow
close together
There were snakes in the jungle.

Kk

keep (verb): **keeps, keeping, kept**
If you keep something, you do not give it away or throw it away.
I kept all her letters.

key (noun)
a thin metal object that you use to lock doors
Where's the front door key?

keyboard (noun)
a part of a computer with letters and numbers that you press *She spends hours tapping at her keyboard.*

kick (verb): **kicks, kicking, kicked**
to bang something with your foot
I kicked the ball to Gemma.

kill (verb): **kills, killing, killed**
to make someone die *The police want to know who killed her.*

kind (adjective)
Kind people are nice to other people and try to help them. *It was kind of her to make me a cake.*

kind (noun)
a type of thing *What kind of pizza do you like best?*

king (noun)
the most senior royal man in a country *King George died in 1936.*

kitchen (noun)
a room where you cook food *Louis is in the kitchen, doing the washing up.*

knee (noun)
the middle part of your leg, where it bends *Harry fell over and cut his knee.*

knife (noun): **knives**
a sharp metal object, used for cutting things *I need a sharp knife to cut the meat.*

knock (verb): **knocks, knocking, knocked** to hit something or bang against something *He knocked on the door.*

know (verb): **knows, knowing, knew, known** to have facts about something in your mind *Do you know that man's name?*

a
b
c
d
e
f
g
h
i
j
k
l
m
n
o
p
q
r
s
t
u
v
w
x
y
z

a
b
c
d
e
f
g
h
i
j
k
l
m
n
o
p
q
r
s
t
u
v
w
x
y
z

Ll

lake (noun)
an area of water with land all around it *We went swimming in the lake.*

lamp (noun)
an electric light that you put on a table *He turned on the lamp next to his bed.*

language (noun)
the words you speak and write *Izzie speaks three languages.*

large (adjective)
big *a large dog*

last (adjective)
the most recent *Our last holiday was in China.*

last (adverb)
after everyone or everything else *Becky came last in the race.*

late (adjective, adverb)
after the right time *Dad was late for work.*

laugh (verb): **laughs, laughing, laughed** to make a noise that shows you think something is funny *His jokes really made us laugh.*

law (noun)
an official rule that a country has *It's against the law to text while you're driving.*

lazy (adjective)
Lazy people do not want to work or make an effort with anything. *He's too lazy to clean his shoes.*

lead (verb): **leads, leading, led** to go in front of someone to show them the way *He led us to an upstairs room.*

leaf (noun): **leaves** the flat green part of a plant *The leaves were beginning to turn red.*

lean (verb): **leans, leaning, leaned** to stand with part of your body against something *Helen leaned against the wall.*

learn (verb): **learns, learning, learned or learnt** to get knowledge about something *We learned about fractions in maths today.*

leave (verb): **leaves, leaving, left**
to go away from a place *The train leaves in five minutes.*

left (adjective, adverb)
on the side of your body where your heart is *Turn left at the traffic lights.*

leg (noun)
one of the parts of your body that you walk with *Can you stand on one leg?*

lemon (noun)
a yellow fruit with a sour taste *I put a slice of lemon in her drink.*

lemonade (noun)
a drink made with lemons and sugar *a glass of lemonade*

lend (verb): **lends, lending, lent**
to let someone use something that belongs to you *Can you lend me a pen?*

lesson (noun)
a period of time when you learn something from a teacher *Gavin fell asleep in the history lesson.*

let (verb): **lets, letting, let**
to allow someone to do something *Mum let us stay up late.*

let's (phrase)
something you say when you want to suggest an activity *Let's go swimming.*

letter (noun)
1. a symbol such as **A**, **b**, **P** or **s** that you use to write words *What letter does "ceiling" start with?*
2. a message on a piece of paper that you send in the post *I got a letter from Abi.*

library (noun): **libraries**
a place where you go to borrow books *I must take this book back to the library.*

lie (verb)
1. **lies, lying, lay, lain**
to be in a position where your body is on a flat surface *He was lying on the floor.*
2. **lies, lying, lied** to say something that is not true *He lied about the money.*

lift (verb): **lifts, lifting, lifted**
to move something to a higher position *Can you help me lift this?*

a
b
c
d
e
f
g
h
i
j
k
l
m
n
o
p
q
r
s
t
u
v
w
x
y
z

a
b
c
d
e
f
g
h
i
j
k
l
m
n
o
p
q
r
s
t
u
v
w
x
y
z

lift (noun)
1. If you give someone a lift, you take them somewhere in your car.
She gave me a lift to the station.
2. something that takes you up and down tall buildings
We took the lift up to the top floor.

light (adjective)
not heavy *The boxes were very light.*

light (noun)
an object that makes a place bright
Can you turn the light on, please?

like (preposition)
similar to *Danny is like his father.*

like (verb): **likes, liking, liked**
to think that something is good or enjoyable *I don't like swimming.*

line (noun)
a long, thin mark
Draw a line from point A to point B.

lion (noun)
a large wild animal from the cat family, with dark yellow fur
The lions sat under a tree.

lip (noun)
one of the two red parts around your mouth *He saw the cake and licked his lips.*

list (noun)
words or phrases written one below the other *We made a shopping list.*

listen (verb): **listens, listening, listened** to give your attention to a sound *I enjoy listening to music.*

little (adjective)
small *He has a little cottage in the country.*

little: a little (determiner, pronoun)
a small amount *"Would you like some cake?" "Just a little, please."*

live (verb): **lives, living, lived**
to have your house somewhere
Keiko lives in Tokyo.

living room (noun)
the room in your house with a sofa, armchairs, etc. *They were in the living room, watching TV.*

lizard (noun)
a small animal that usually lives in hot places and has thick, rough skin

lock (verb): **locks, locking, locked**
to fasten a door with a key
Make sure you lock the door when you leave.

long (adjective)
when one end is far from the other
long hair

look (verb): **looks, looking, looked**
1. to use your eyes to see something
Look at the lions!
2. to seem to be
That pizza looks delicious!

look after (verb): **looks after, looking after, looked after**
to take care of someone *I have to look after my little brother tomorrow.*

lorry (noun): **lorries**
a large vehicle for carrying things
A big lorry carries the potatoes from the farm.

lose (verb): **loses, losing, lost**
to not be able to find something
Dad's always losing his glasses.

lot: a lot of, lots of (determiner)
many *Lara has a lot of friends. ; I ate lots of cake.*

lot: a lot, lots (pronoun)
many or a large amount *Would you like some sweets? There are lots here.*

loud (adjective)
A loud sound is noisy and easy to hear. *Our teacher has a very loud voice.*

love (verb): **loves, loving, loved**
to like someone or something very much *I really love my parents.*

lovely (adjective)
very nice, beautiful or enjoyable
We had a lovely time at the party.

low (adjective)
not high *a low fence*

lucky (adjective)
If you are lucky, good things happen to you by chance. *We were very lucky to escape from the fire.*

lunch (noun): **lunches**
the meal you have in the middle of the day *I had soup for lunch.*

a
b
c
d
e
f
g
h
i
j
k
l
m
n
o
p
q
r
s
t
u
v
w
x
y
z

a
b
c
d
e
f
g
h
i
j
k
l
m
n
o
p
q
r
s
t
u
v
w
x
y
z

Mm

magazine (noun)
a type of book
with large pages
and a soft cover
that you buy every
week or month
a fashion magazine

magic (noun)
something that makes impossible
things happen *She used her magic
to turn the frog into a prince.*

magician (noun)
someone who does magic tricks
I had a magician at my party.

make (verb): **makes, making,
made** to create something *I made
a birthday card for my friend.*

make sure (verb)
to do something so that you are
certain that something will happen
Make sure that the door is locked.

man (noun): **men**
an adult male *Who is that man
with the black hat?*

manage (verb): **manages,
managing, managed**
to be able to do something difficult
I managed to get there in time.

mango (noun): **mangoes**
a very sweet fruit that grows in hot
countries, and has green skin and
an orange part that you eat
We ate some juicy mangoes.

map (noun)
a drawing that
shows where
places such as
towns, roads
and rivers are
We could see the lake on the map.

mark (noun)
a letter or number that tells you how
good your work is *What mark did
you get for your maths test?*

mark (verb): **marks, marking,
marked** When teachers mark
your work, they give you a number
or letter to show how well you have
done it. *Miss Church hasn't marked
our homework yet.*

market (noun)
a place where people go to buy and
sell things *We buy our vegetables at
the market.*

married (adjective)
A married person has a husband or wife. *When are you going to get married?*

mat (noun)
a flat piece of cloth that you put on the floor *Wipe your shoes on the mat.*

match (noun): **matches**
a sports game *a hockey match*

math (noun)
the American word for "maths"

maths (noun)
the study of numbers *We have a new maths teacher.*

meal (noun)
food that you eat, especially breakfast, lunch or dinner *We have our main meal in the evening.*

mean (verb): **means, meaning, meant** to have a particular meaning *What does "fabric" mean?*

meat (noun)
food made from pieces of animals' bodies *Vegetarians don't eat meat.*

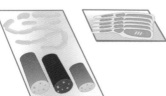

medicine (noun)
a liquid that makes you better when you are ill *Mum gave me some cough medicine.*

meet (verb): **meets, meeting, met** to come to the same place as someone you have arranged to see *I'll meet you by the church.*

meeting (noun)
a time when people arrange to come together to talk about something *They had a meeting to discuss the problem.*

member (noun)
someone who belongs to a group or club *She's a member of the orchestra.*

message (noun)
information that one person gives to another person *Can you give Jack a message from me?*

metal (noun)
a hard, shiny substance such as iron or silver *They keep the oil in metal containers.*

metre (noun)
a unit of measurement equal to 100 centimetres *about five metres long*

middle (adjective, noun)
the centre of something *The cake has jam in the middle.*

a
b
c
d
e
f
g
h
i
j
k
l
m
n
o
p
q
r
s
t
u
v
w
x
y
z

a
b
c
d
e
f
g
h
i
j
k
l

m

n
o
p
q
r
s
t
u
v
w
x
y
z

midnight (noun)
12 o'clock at night
The clock struck midnight.

milk (noun)
a white liquid from cows, that people drink *Do you have milk in your tea?*

million (noun)
the number 1,000,000
Their house cost over a million pounds.

mind (verb): **minds, minding, minded** to be upset or cross about something *Do you mind if I open the window?*

minute (noun)
a period of 60 seconds
Boil the egg for four minutes.

mirror (noun)
a glass object that you use for looking at yourself *I checked my hair in the mirror.*

miss (verb): **misses, missing, missed**
1. to feel sad because you are not with someone *My friend moved away and I really miss him.*
2. If you miss a plane, train, etc., you are too late to catch it.
I missed my bus this morning.

mistake (noun)
something that you say, think or do that is not correct *I made lots of mistakes in my maths homework.*

mix (verb): **mixes, mixing, mixed**
to combine two or more substances so that they become one substance *Mix the butter with the sugar.*

moment (noun)
a very short period of time
Please wait for a moment.

money (noun)
the coins and paper notes that we use to pay for things *I've earned enough money to buy a new bike.*

monkey (noun)
a wild animal that has a long tail and climbs trees

monster (noun)
an ugly, frightening creature in stories *The monster lived in a cave.*

month (noun)
a period of about 30 days
I start my new school next month.

moon (noun)
the round object that shines in the sky at night
The moon is very bright tonight.

more (adverb, pronoun, determiner)
a bigger amount or an extra amount
Would you like some more cake?

morning (noun)
the time between the end of the
night and the afternoon
I go for a run every morning.

most (adverb, pronoun, determiner)
the biggest amount or nearly all
of something *Gerry scored the
most points.*

mother (noun)
your parent who is a woman
My mother is a scientist.

motorbike (noun)
a vehicle that
looks like a
big bicycle
with an engine
My brother rides a motorbike.

mountain (noun)
a very high hill *Mount Everest is
the highest mountain in the world.*

mouse (noun)
1. mice or mouses a small object
that you move with your hand to
control a computer
Use the mouse to click on the icon.
2. mice a small furry
animal with a long tail
Joe has a pet mouse.

moustache (noun)
hair that some men grow above
their mouth *My dad has grown
a moustache.*

mouth (noun)
the part of your
face that you
eat and speak with
Don't put your fingers in your mouth.

move (verb): **moves, moving,
moved** to change position
Suddenly, the lion moved.

movie (noun)
the American word for "film"
*I like to watch funny movies with
my friends.*

much (adverb, pronoun, determiner)
a large amount *We don't have
much money.*

mum, mummy (noun)
a child's word for "mother"
My mum takes me to school.

museum (noun)
a place where people go to see
interesting objects *We went to
the science museum.*

music (noun)
sounds made by instruments or
singing *What kind of music do
you like?*

a
b
c
d
e
f
g
h
i
j
k
l
m
n
o
p
q
r
s
t
u
v
w
x
y
z

Nn

name (noun)
what someone or something is called
His name is Ivan.

narrow (adjective)
a very small distance from one side
to the other *a narrow street*

naughty (adjective)
Naughty children behave badly.
"Stop being naughty!"

near (adverb, preposition)
not far away, close *We lived near
the river.*

necessary (adjective)
needed *It is necessary to wear
a helmet.*

neck (noun)
the part of your body that joins your
head to your body *She had a scarf
around her neck.*

necklace (noun)
a piece of jewellery that
you wear around your
neck *a pink necklace.*

need (verb): **needs, needing,
needed** If you need something, you
have to have it. *I need a new coat.*

neighbour (noun)
someone who lives next door to
you or very near you *One of our
neighbours has a parrot.*

neither (adjective, adverb, pronoun)
not even one of two things
Neither of the keys fit this lock.

new (adjective)
made or bought recently
I've got a new bike.

news (noun)
information about things that are
happening in the world *My city has
been in the news again.*

newspaper (noun)
a set of large pieces
of paper with the
news printed on them
*Mum likes to read the
newspaper at breakfast time.*

next (adjective, adverb)
immediately following *When's your
next football match?*

next to (preposition)
very close, with nothing in between
I stood next to my brother.

nice (adjective)
pleasant, enjoyable or kind
Our new teacher is really nice.

night (noun)
the time when it is dark
There was a big storm in the night.

nobody, no one (pronoun)
not one person *Nobody knew the answer.*

nod (verb): **nods, nodding, nodded**
to move your head up and down to
say yes *I asked if he was hungry
and he nodded.*

noise (noun)
loud sounds *Our dishwasher makes
a lot of noise.*

noisy (adjective)
making a lot of noise *The children
were very noisy.*

none (determiner, pronoun)
not one *None of the lifts
were working.*

normal (adjective)
like most other people or things;
ordinary *It's normal to feel
angry sometimes.*

north (noun)
the direction at the top of a map
They live in the north of China.

nose (noun)
the part of your face that
you use to smell *My
uncle has a big nose.*

note (noun)
a short written message
I left a note for my mum.

notice (verb): **notices, noticing,
noticed** to become aware of
something by seeing, hearing or
feeling it *I noticed a strange smell in
the room.*

now (adverb)
at this moment *Now we're going
to do some singing.*

nowhere (adverb)
not any place *There's nowhere to
sit down.*

number (noun)
one of the symbols such as 1, 2, 3
that we use for counting *They live
at number 120 Mill Road.*

nurse (noun)
someone who looks after sick people
as their job *The nurse gave Erik an
injection.*

nut (noun)
a small, brown, dry
fruit that grows on trees
Walnuts are my favourite type of nut.

a
b
c
d
e
f
g
h
i
j
k
l
m
n
o
p
q
r
s
t
u
v
w
x
y
z

Oo

a b c d e f g h i j k l m n o p q r s t u v w x y z

o'clock (adverb)
something that you say after a number to say what time it is *Let's meet at 3 o'clock.*

octopus (noun): **octopuses**
an animal with eight long legs that lives in the sea

of course (phrase)
something that you say to agree strongly *"Could you help me with these bags?" "Yes, of course."*

offer (verb): **offers, offering, offered** to ask someone if they would like something *I offered her a piece of cake.*

office (noun)
a room where people work *She gets to the office at 9 a.m.*

oil (noun)
a thick black liquid that is used as fuel or to make parts work smoothly *You need some oil on your bike chain.*

OK (adjective)
good or good enough *The film was OK.*

OK (exclamation)
something that you say to agree to something *OK, you can come with us if you want to.*

old (adjective)
An old person or thing has existed for a long time. *We have a very old dog called Chester.*

once (adverb)
one time *I visit my grandma once a week.*

onion (noun)
a round vegetable with thin dry skin and layers inside that taste very strong *We had fried onions with our burgers.*

online (adjective, adverb)
connected to the internet *I do a lot of my shopping online.*

open (adjective)
1. not closed *The door was open.*
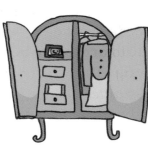
2. If a shop, museum, etc., is open, you can go in. *Is the museum open on Sundays?*

open (verb): **opens, opening, opened** If you open a door or a window, you move it so that it is not closed. *It's hot in here – let's open the window.*

opinion (noun)
Your opinion is what you think about something. *What was your opinion of the film?*

opportunity (noun): **opportunities**
a chance for you to do something *You will have plenty of opportunity to ask questions.*

opposite (preposition)
facing something that is on the other side *Suri is sitting opposite Yuko.*

orange (adjective)
the colour made by mixing red and yellow *She wore an orange dress.*

orange (noun)
a juicy, round, orange fruit *a glass of orange juice*

order (verb): **orders, ordering, ordered**
1. to arrange things in a particular way *The documents are ordered by date.*
2. to tell someone in a strict way that they must do something *The police officer ordered us to move away.*

ordinary (adjective)
not special or unusual *I just want an ordinary bike, not a racing bike.*

organize (verb): **organizes, organizing, organized**
to arrange an activity or an event *We organized a big party for Mum.*

outside (adverb, preposition)
not inside something *Go and wait outside the headteacher's office.*

outside (noun)
the outer part of something *The outside of the house is very ugly.*

oven (noun)
something you use in a kitchen to cook food *Put the cake in the oven.*

over (adverb, preposition)
1. above or from one side to the other *They jumped over the stream.*
2. more than *There were over 50 people in the room.*

owe (verb): **owes, owing, owed**
If you owe money to someone, you have to pay it back to them. *Ricky owes me money.*

own (verb): **own, owning, owned**
If you own something, it belongs to you. *Who owns that palace?*

a
b
c
d
e
f
g
h
i
j
k
l
m
n
o
p
q
r
s
t
u
v
w
x
y
z

a b c d e f g h i j k l m n o **p** q r s t u v w x y z

Pp

pack (verb): **packs, packing, packed** to put clothes into a suitcase *Have you packed your trainers?*

page (noun)
one of the pieces of paper in a book *Turn to page seven.*

paint (noun)
a coloured liquid that you use to make pictures or to decorate walls *We bought yellow paint for the living room.*

paint (verb): **paints, painting, painted** to make a picture or decorate a room using paint *Joe painted a picture of the sea.*

painting (noun)
a picture made with paint *A painting of some mountains hung above the fireplace.*

pair (noun)
two things that go together *a pair of shoes*

panda (noun)
a large animal from China, with black and white fur

paper (noun)
a thin, flat material that you write on *Write your answers on a piece of paper.*

parcel (noun)
something that is wrapped in paper so that it can be sent in the post *The game came in a big parcel.*

parent (noun)
your mother or father *My parents bought me a new bike.*

park (noun)
an outdoor area where you go to play *We played football in the park.*

parrot (noun)
a large bird with brightly coloured feathers *Our parrot can say "Hello".*

part (noun)
one piece of something *Part of the zoo was closed.*

party (noun): **parties**
an event where people meet to have fun by talking, dancing, eating, etc. *a birthday party*

pass (verb): **passes, passing, passed**
1. to go past something or someone *I passed Mr Collins on my way to school.*
2. If you pass an exam, you are successful. *Charlie passed his piano exam.*

passenger (noun)
someone who travels on a bus, train, etc. *The taxi was carrying three passengers.*

passport (noun)
a document that looks like a small book, that you need to travel from one country to another *The man checked our passports before we got on the plane.*

past (noun)
all the time that has already existed *In the past, many houses didn't have bathrooms.*

past (preposition)
If you go past something, you go by it on your way to another place. *I saw Anna walk past our house.*

pasta (noun)
an Italian food made from flour, water and sometimes eggs, made into different shapes *We had pasta with tomato sauce.*

path (noun)
a long, narrow area of ground that people walk along to get from one place to another *The path lead us into a forest.*

patient (adjective)
If you are patient, you don't mind if things take a long time or if other people do annoying things. *Our teacher is very patient when we don't understand his lesson.*

patient (noun)
someone who is being treated by a doctor or nurse *She advises all her patients to take exercise.*

a
b
c
d
e
f
g
h
i
j
k
l
m
n
o
p
q
r
s
t
u
v
w
x
y
z

pattern (noun)
a repeated design of lines or shapes
The curtains have a pattern of coloured circles.

pea (noun)
a small, round green vegetable

pear (noun)
a fruit that has green skin and is white inside

pen (noun)
an object that you use for writing with ink
Make sure you bring a pen and a pencil.

pencil (noun)
an object that you use for writing or drawing
coloured pencils

pepper (noun)
1. a grey powder with a hot flavour, that you put in food
Add salt and pepper to the soup.
2. a green, red, yellow or orange vegetable that you can eat raw or cooked

perfect (adjective)
as good as possible *This is the perfect place for a holiday!*

perform (verb): **performs, performing, performed**
to act, sing, etc., in front of other people *She performed her new song.*

perhaps (adverb)
something that you say to show that something might be true or might happen *Perhaps we'll see a lion.*

person (noun): **people, persons**
a baby, child or adult *How many people are coming to your party?*

persuade (verb): **persuades, persuading, persuaded**
to try to make someone do something *I persuaded Dad to let me stay up late.*

pet (noun)
an animal that you keep at home
a pet rabbit

petrol (noun)
a liquid that you put in a car to make it go *We almost ran out of petrol.*

phone (noun)
something that you use to speak to someone in a different place
a mobile phone

phone (verb): **phones, phoning, phoned** to speak to somebody on the phone *I need to phone your mum.*

photo (noun)
a picture that is made with a camera *Frankie took a photo of the horse.*

piano (noun)
a large musical instrument with black and white parts that you press *Do you play the piano?*

pick up (verb): **picks up, picking up, picked up**
to lift something off a surface with your hand *Millie picked up the book and started to read.*

picnic (noun)
a meal that you take to eat outside *We had a picnic in the park.*

picture (noun)
a painting, drawing or photo *Hamza drew a picture of a dog.*

pie (noun)
a food made of pastry with meat, fruit, etc., inside *apple pie*

piece (noun)
a part of something *a piece of cake*

pig (noun)
a pink farm animal with a fat body and short legs

pilot (noun)
someone whose job is to fly planes *The pilot told us to fasten our seat belts.*

pineapple (noun)
a large, very sweet fruit that grows in hot countries and is yellow inside *pineapple juice*

pink (adjective)
the colour that is made by mixing red and white *a pink dress*

pirate (noun)
someone who attacks ships and steals things from them

pizza (noun)
a flat, round piece of bread with tomatoes, melted cheese and often other types of food on top *a pepperoni pizza*

place (noun)
a position or area *Mexico City is a very big place.*

a
b
c
d
e
f
g
h
i
j
k
l
m
n
o
p
q
r
s
t
u
v
w
x
y
z

plan (noun)
something that you have decided to do *We thought of a plan to make some money.*

plane (noun)
a vehicle with wings that you fly in *Our plane landed in Hong Kong at 6 p.m.*

planet (noun)
a large round object in space that moves around the sun or a different star *Mars and Venus are the planets closest to Earth.*

plant (noun)
something that has leaves and roots and grows in the ground *We bought some tomato plants.*

plant (verb): **plants, planting, planted**
to put seeds or a plant into the ground *We planted some sunflowers in the garden.*

plastic (adjective, noun)
a strong, light substance that can be made into different shapes and is used to make many things *a plastic bottle*

plate (noun)
a flat object that you put food on before you eat it *a plate of sandwiches*

play (verb): **plays, playing, played**
to do a sport or a game *They played tennis.*

playground (noun)
an area next to a school where students can play *The children ran around in the playground.*

please (exclamation)
something that you say to ask for something politely *Could you help me, please?*

pleased (adjective)
happy about something *Sophie looked pleased with her present.*

plenty (adjective, noun)
as much as you need and maybe more *There was plenty of food for everyone.*

p.m. (abbreviation)
in the afternoon or evening *We finish school at 3 p.m.*

pocket (noun)
a part of
a piece of
clothing that
is like a small
bag where you
can put things
Put the pen in my shirt pocket.

poem (noun)
a piece of writing, often with short lines that end with words that sound the same *Leanne wrote a poem about autumn.*

point (verb): **points, pointing, pointed** to hold your finger out towards something in order to show someone where it is *Clara pointed at the painting.*

police (noun)
people whose job is to try to catch criminals *I think you should call the police.*

police officer (noun)
someone who works for the police *The police officers told us to move back.*

poor (adjective)
Poor people have a very small amount of money. *His grandparents were too poor to buy a TV.*

popular (adjective)
If a person or a thing is popular, lots of people like them. *Curtis is one of the most popular boys in my class.*

position (noun)
the place where something is, or the way that it is placed *We changed the position of the chairs.*

positive (adjective)
A positive person feels happy about life and expects good things to happen. *Freddie has a very positive attitude to his school work.*

possible (adjective)
If something is possible, it might happen or be true. *It's not possible to learn a language that quickly.*

post (verb): **posts, posting, posted** to send a letter or a parcel *I posted the letter yesterday.*

postcard (noun)
a card with a picture on one side that you send someone when you are on holiday *Rory sent us a postcard from Toronto.*

post office (noun)
a place where you can post letters and parcels, buy stamps, etc. *Our town has four post offices.*

a
b
c
d
e
f
g
h
i
j
k
l
m
n
o
p
q
r
s
t
u
v
w
x
y
z

a
b
c
d
e
f
g
h
i
j
k
l
m
n
o
p
q
r
s
t
u
v
w
x
y
z

potato (noun): **potatoes**
a round vegetable
that grows in the
ground and is
white inside
*We had baked
potatoes for tea.*

pour (verb): **pours, pouring,
poured** to tip liquid out of a
container *He poured boiling water
on to the teabag.*

practise (verb): **practises,
practising, practised** to do
something again and again so that
you get better at it *I need to practise
singing this song.*

prefer (verb): **prefers, preferring,
preferred** to like one thing better
than another *Do you prefer tennis or
volleyball?*

prepare (verb): **prepares,
preparing, prepared**
to get something ready *Mum
prepared the spare room for
our guest.*

present (noun)
1. something that you
give someone; gift
a birthday present
2. something that is
happening now *The play is
set in the present day.*

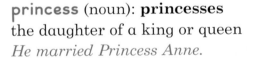

president (noun)
the leader of the government in
some countries *He is president of
the United States of America.*

press (verb): **presses, pressing,
pressed** to push something
He pressed the button on the lift.

pretty (adjective)
a pretty girl or woman has a face
that looks nice *Your sister's
really pretty.*

prince (noun)
the son of
a king or
queen
*She was
excited to
meet Prince Harry.*

princess (noun): **princesses**
the daughter of a king or queen
He married Princess Anne.

prison (noun)
a place where criminals are kept
as a punishment *The thief was
sent to prison.*

prisoner (noun)
a person who is in prison
*The king decided to set the
prisoners free.*

private (adjective)
only for one person or group of people and not for everybody
The hotel has a private beach.

prize (noun)
something that you get if you win a competition
Ted won first prize in the school poetry competition.

probably (adverb)
If you say that something is probably true, you think it is likely to be true but you are not sure.
It will probably rain later.

problem (noun)
something that causes a difficulty
I've got a problem with my laptop – it keeps turning off.

programme (noun)
a TV or radio show *I love watching programmes about animals.*

promise (verb): **promises, promising, promised**
to say that you will definitely do something *Dad promised to mend my bike today.*

protect (verb): **protects, protecting, protected**
to make sure that someone or something stays safe *Conor's big brother tries to protect him at school.*

proud (adjective)
pleased about something you own or something you have done
Lola was very proud of being in the gymnastics team.

prove (verb): **proves, proving, proved** to show that something is true *I can prove I was in London on that day.*

pull (verb): **pulls, pulling, pulled** to move something with your hands, usually towards you *She was pulling a small suitcase behind her.*

purple (adjective)
the colour made by mixing red and blue
The queen was wearing a purple dress.

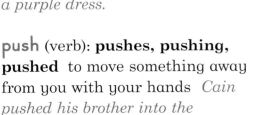

push (verb): **pushes, pushing, pushed** to move something away from you with your hands *Cain pushed his brother into the swimming pool.*

put (verb): **puts, putting, put** to move something to a particular position *Grace put the books on the shelf.*

put on (verb): **puts on, putting on, put on** to start to wear clothes *I put my coat on.*

a
b
c
d
e
f
g
h
i
j
k
l
m
n
o
p
q
r
s
t
u
v
w
x
y
z

Qq

quarter (noun)
one of four equal parts
of something

queen (noun)
the most senior royal
woman in a country
*Queen Victoria died
in 1901.*

question (noun)
the words that you ask someone
when you want an answer
Do you have any questions?

quick (adjective)
Something that is quick does not
take a very long time.
Can I ask a quick question?

quiet (adjective)
If a person or a thing is quiet, they
do not make a lot of noise. If a place
is quiet, there are not any loud
noises there. *Can everyone be
quiet, please?*

quite (adverb)
fairly, but not very *I'm quite hungry
but I can wait.*

Rr

rabbit (noun)
a small animal
with soft fur and
long ears *a pet rabbit*

race (noun)
a competition to find out which
person or animal can run the fastest
*Ben came first in the running race at
sports day.*

race (verb): **races, racing, raced**
to run to a place *The children
raced to the park.*

rain (noun)
drops of water
that fall from
clouds in the sky
*It was raining so
I took my umbrella.*

rain (verb):
**rains, raining,
rained**
When it rains,
drops of water
fall from clouds
in the sky.

rainbow (noun)
a curved shape that appears in the sky when the sun shines on rain. It is made of many different colours.

read (verb): **reads, reading, read**
to look at words on a page and understand them *I like reading stories in bed.*

ready (adjective)
able to do something immediately *Are you ready to leave yet?*

real (adjective)
Real things and people actually exist. *He's not real. He's just a boy in a story.*

realize (verb): **realizes, realizing, realized** to understand or start to know something *We realized we were lost.*

really (adverb)
very *It's really hot today.*

receive (verb): **receives, receiving, received** to get something
I received lots of cards on my birthday.

recognize (verb): **recognizes, recognizing, recognized**
to know someone because you have seen them before *I didn't recognize her because she has changed her hairstyle.*

red (adjective)
the colour of blood
Red is my favourite colour.

refuse (verb): **refuses, refusing, refused** to say that you don't want to do something *Mum refused to buy us any sweets.*

regular (adjective)
Something that is regular happens often or at the same time every day, week, etc. *Regular visits to the dentist are important.*

relative (noun)
someone in your family *We usually visit relatives on Sundays.*

remember (verb): **remembers, remembering, remembered**
1. to think about someone or something from the past
Do you remember your first holiday?
2. to keep something in your mind
I must remember to do my homework tonight.

a
b
c
d
e
f
g
h
i
j
k
l
m
n
o
p
q
r
s
t
u
v
w
x
y
z

rent (verb): **rents, renting, rented**
If you rent an apartment, you pay money to the owner so that you can live in it.

repair (verb): **repairs, repairing, repaired** to fix something that is broken
Can you help me repair my car?

repeat (verb): **repeats, repeating, repeated** to do or say something again *Could you repeat that, please?*

rest (verb): **rests, resting, rested** to stop working and lie down or relax *You look tired. You should rest.*

restaurant (noun)
a place where you pay to eat food *Do you know any good restaurants near here?*

return (verb): **returns, returning, returned** to go back to a place *He went away and never returned.*

rice (noun)
a type of food made of small white seeds. You cook them in water and they become soft. *We had fish, rice and peas for dinner.*

rich (adjective)
Rich people have a lot of money. *Anna's parents are very rich.*

ride (verb): **rides, riding, rode, ridden** If you ride a bicycle or a horse, you sit on it and move along. *Can you ride a bike?*

right (adjective)
correct *Well done – that's the right answer!*

ring (verb): **rings, ringing, rang, rung** to make the sound of a bell *The doorbell rang.*

river (noun)
a long stream of water that moves towards the sea *What's the longest river in the world?*

road (noun)
a wide path with a hard surface that cars travel on *It's safe to cross the road here.*

robot (noun)
a machine that can do the same work as humans

rock (noun)
a large stone on the ground or in the sea *The boat crashed on the rocks.*

rocket (noun)
a large tube with a pointed end that travels in space

roof (noun)
the top part of a house that covers it

room (noun)
a part in a building that has walls and a ceiling *the living room*

rose (noun)
a flower with sharp points on its stem

rough (adjective)
not smooth to touch
Elephants have rough skin.

round (adjective)
in the shape of a circle
a round window

round (adverb)
1. Something goes round when it turns like a wheel.
The wheels went round very fast.
2. You turn round when you move to face in the opposite direction.
She turned round and saw a boy.

row (noun)
a line of things or people
We sat in the front row of the cinema.

rubber (noun)
an object that you use for removing pencil marks

rubbish (noun)
things that you don't want any more
Put your rubbish in the bin, please.

ruler (noun)
a long flat piece of plastic that you use for drawing straight lines and for measuring things

run (verb): **runs, running, ran, run** to use your legs to move very fast
I can run very fast.

a
b
c
d
e
f
g
h
i
j
k
l
m
n
o
p
q
r
s
t
u
v
w
x
y
z

Ss

sad (adjective)
not happy *We were sad to say goodbye.*

safe (adjective)
not in danger *The children are safe at home with their father.*

salad (noun)
a mixture of vegetables that you eat cold
a salad of lettuce, tomato and onions

salt (noun)
white powder that you can put on food to make it taste better
Could you pass the salt, please?

same (adjective, pronoun)
not different
Maria and Eva are wearing the same shoes!

sand (noun)
yellow or pale brown powder that covers the ground of a beach
We play on the sand and swim in the sea.

sandwich (noun): **sandwiches**
a snack of cheese, meat, egg, etc., between two slices of bread
a cheese sandwich

sausage (noun)
a food made of chopped meat in a thin tube *We bought sausages to make hot dogs.*

save (verb): **saves, saving, saved**
to take someone out of danger
Thank you – you saved me!

say (verb): **says, saying, said**
to speak words *What did you say?*

scarf (noun): **scarves**
a long piece of clothing that you wear around your neck

school (noun)
a place where young people go to learn *Do you go to school on Saturdays?*

science (noun)
the study of animals, plants, metals, water, air and heat *Science is my favourite subject at school.*

scissors (plural noun)
a tool that you use to cut paper

score (noun)
the number of points that a team wins in a game *The score was 4–2.*

score (verb): **scores, scoring, scored** to win a point in a game such as football *George scored the winning goal.*

scream (verb): **screams, screaming, screamed** to make a long high sound because you are frightened or in pain *The girl screamed in pain.*

screen (noun)
the front surface of a mobile phone or TV *Tap the screen here to open the app.*

sea (noun)
the salt water that covers large parts of the Earth *We like swimming in the sea.*

seat (noun)
something that you sit on *There aren't enough seats for everyone.*

second (adjective)
A second thing comes after the first thing. *My sister is in her second year at college.*

second (noun)
a very short amount of time *Can you wait a second, please?*

secret (noun)
something that you must not tell to anyone else *Can I tell you a secret?*

see (verb): **sees, seeing, saw, seen** to notice something with your eyes *Can you see that house at the top of the hill?*

sell (verb): **sells, selling, sold** to give something to someone for money *My dad wants to sell his car.*

send (verb): **sends, sending, sent** to have a written message delivered to someone *We sent Grandpa a birthday card.*

sentence (noun)
a group of words that someone says or writes *A sentence starts with a capital letter and ends with a full stop.*

serious (adjective)
A serious person does not laugh or smile very much.

several (adjective)
more than two, but not many *Several people arrived early.*

a
b
c
d
e
f
g
h
i
j
k
l
m
n
o
p
q
r
s
t
u
v
w
x
y
z

shake (verb): **shakes, shaking, shook, shaken** to move quickly from side to side or up and down
The house shakes every time a train passes by.

share (verb): **shares, sharing, shared** to each take a part of something *The children shared the cake between them.*

shark (noun)
a large sea fish with a lot of sharp teeth

sheep (noun): **sheep**
a white or black animal that farmers keep for its wool and meat

shelf (noun): **shelves**
a long flat piece of wood or metal that is fixed to a wall, used for storing books, etc.
a book shelf

shell (noun)
the hard covering of an egg, a nut or a small sea animal

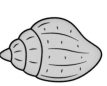

shield (noun)
an object that soldiers used to carry to protect themselves

shirt (noun)
a piece of clothing with a collar and buttons that you wear on the top part of your body
Dad wears a shirt and tie when he's at the office.

shoe (noun)
You wear shoes to cover and protect your feet when you go outside.
Please take your shoes off before you come in.

shop (noun)
a place where you can buy things
There's a small shop on the corner of our street.

shopping (noun)
You go shopping when you go to the shops and buy things.
We go shopping every Saturday morning.

short (adjective)
not long *a short story*

shorts (plural noun)
short trousers that end above the knee

a b c d e f g h i j k l m n o p q r s t u v w x y z

shoulder (noun)
the part of your body at the top of your arm

shout (verb): **shouts, shouting, shouted** to say something in a loud voice *The boy was shouting "Help me!"*

show (verb): **shows, showing, showed, shown** to let people see something *Show me your new football boots!*

shower (noun)
an object in the bathroom that you stand under to wash yourself *I take a shower every morning.*

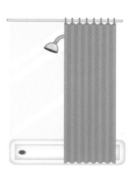

shut (verb): **shuts, shutting, shut** to close something *Shut the door, please!*

shy (adjective)
A shy person does not like talking to new people. *Don't be shy!*

sick (adjective)
not feeling very well *"Where's John?" "He's sick today."*

side (noun)
one of the surfaces of an object *A cube has six sides.*

sign (noun)
a board or notice with writing on it *a road sign*

silver (noun)
a pale grey metal that is used for making rings, necklaces, bracelets, and so on *a silver bracelet*

sing (verb): **sings, singing, sang, sung** to make music with your voice *We sing songs in the car.*

singer (noun)
a person who sings *Who is your favourite singer?*

sister (noun)
a girl who has the same parents as you *I have a brother and three sisters.*

sit (verb): **sits, sitting, sat** to rest yourself on a chair *Come and sit next to me.*

size (noun)
how big something is *What size shoes do you take?*

skate (verb): **skates, skating, skated** to move along on ice wearing special boots with blades on the bottom *Can you skate?*

a b c d e f g h i j k l m n o p q r **s** t u v w x y z

ski (verb): **skis, skiing, skied**
to move along on snow wearing skis
(long narrow strips of metal)
I learned to ski last winter.

skirt (noun)
a piece of clothing
that hangs around
your waist

sky (noun): **skies**
the area above the Earth where
you can see clouds, the sun and the
moon *blue sky*

sleep (verb):
**sleeps, sleeping,
slept**
to close your
eyes and rest,
usually at night
Shhhh! The baby is sleeping now.

slow (adjective)
not fast or quick *a slow train*

slowly (adverb)
not fast or quickly *Grandpa walks
very slowly.*

small (adjective)
not big *These shoes are too small
for me.*

smell (noun)
something that you notice with your
nose *What's that horrible smell?*

smell (verb): **smells, smelling,
smelled or smelt** to have a smell
or to notice a smell *Your perfume
smells nice! ; I can smell smoke.*

smile (noun)
the way that you smile
Jenny's got a lovely smile.

smile (verb): **smiles, smiling,
smiled**
to turn the corners
of your mouth
upwards to
show that
you are happy
Jack smiled at me.

snack (noun)
a small, quick meal *If you're hungry,
have a healthy snack.*

snake (noun)
an animal with no legs and
a long narrow body

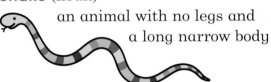

snow (noun)
small pieces of soft ice that fall from
the sky in winter *We love to play
in the snow.*

snow (verb):
snows, snowing, snowed
When it snows, snow falls from
the sky. *Look outside! It's snowing!*

snowball (noun)
a ball of snow that you throw
The children had a snowball fight.

snowboarding (noun)
a sport in which you move along on snow on a wide board
go snowboarding

snowman (noun): **snowmen**
a model of a person that you make using snow *Shall we build a snowman?*

soap (noun)
the stuff that you mix with water to wash with *a bar of soap*

soccer (noun)
the American word for "football"
a game of soccer

sock (noun)
a piece of clothing that you wear on your feet *a pair of socks*

sofa (noun)
a long, soft seat for two or three people

soft (adjective)
not hard *soft skin*

soldier (noun)
someone who fights in wars

somebody, someone (pronoun)
used for talking about a person when you don't know who that person is *Someone has taken my pen!*

something (pronoun)
used for talking about a thing when you don't know what it is
Oh! There's something in my glass of water!

sometimes (adverb)
on some occasions but not always
Sometimes I go to a friend's house for tea.

somewhere (pronoun)
used for talking about a place when you don't know where that place is
I've left my keys somewhere.

son (noun)
someone's male child
Anna has a son and two daughters.

song (noun)
a piece of music that you sing
We always sing songs in the car.

soon (adverb)
in a short time from now
Goodbye, see you soon!

a b c d e f g h i j k l m n o p q r s t u v w x y z

77

a
b
c
d
e
f
g
h
i
j
k
l
m
n
o
p
q
r
s
t
u
v
w
x
y
z

sorry (adjective)
You feel sorry when you feel bad about something. *I'm sorry to hear your sad news.*

sorry (exclamation)
something that you say when you have done something wrong
Sorry, I broke your toy.

sound (noun)
something that you hear
This toy makes a funny sound when you press it.

soup (noun)
a liquid food made with meat or vegetables *a bowl of tomato soup*

south (noun)
the direction at the bottom of the map *She lives in the south of France.*

space (noun)
1. the very large area that all the planets and stars are in
a film about space travel

2. an empty place
There's a space for you to sit here.

speak (verb): **speaks, speaking, spoke, spoken** to say something
Can I speak to Fiona, please?

special (adjective)
not ordinary *Your birthday is a special day.*

spell (noun)
words that make magic happen in stories *The witch put a spell on the princess.*

spell (verb): **spells, spelling, spelled or spelt** to say or write the letters of a word in the correct order *How do you spell your name?*

spend (verb): **spends, spending, spent**
1. to use money to pay for things
Don't spend all your money!
2. to take time doing something
We spent our holiday by the sea.

spider (noun)
a small creature with eight legs

spoon (noun)
an object that you use for eating or serving food such as soup or ice cream *a soup spoon*

sport (noun)
activities like running, cycling and playing basketball, football, etc. *My favourite sport is swimming.*

sports centre (noun)
a place where you go to do sports

spot (noun)
a small round mark *a white dog with black spots*

spring (noun)
the time of year between winter and summer, when many new flowers start to appear *Our garden is beautiful in spring.*

square (noun)
a shape with four straight sides of equal length

stage (noun)
the place in a theatre where the actors stand

stairs (plural noun)
the steps in a building where you go from one level to the next *The lift was broken so we took the stairs.*

stamp (noun)
a small piece of paper with a picture on it that you stick on an envelope before you send it *a first-class stamp*

stand (verb): **stands, standing, stood** to move to an upright position on your feet *We all stand when the teacher comes into the room.*

star (noun)
1. a famous singer or film actor *a film star*
2. one of the bright points of light that you see in the sky at night

station (noun)
a place where trains or buses stop for people to get on or off *I'll meet you at the railway station at midday.*

stay (verb): **stays, staying, stayed** to be in the same place for a period of time *We will stay with you until your mum arrives.*

steal (verb): **steals, stealing, stole, stolen** to take something that is not yours *The thieves stole all our money.*

a b c d e f g h i j k l m n o p q r s t u v w x y z

step (noun)
the flat part of a stair that you put
your foot on to go up or down

still (adjective)
not moving *Please sit still!*

stomach (noun)
the part of your body where your
food goes when you eat it
My stomach hurts!

stone (noun)
a piece of rock (very hard material
that you find on the ground)
Don't throw stones.

stop (verb): **stops, stopping,
stopped** to finish doing something
and not continue *Stop writing
now, please.*

store (noun)
the American word for "shop"

storm (noun)
a period of bad
weather when
there is very
strong wind
and heavy
rain

story (noun): **stories**
a description of imaginary events
Our teacher told us a story.

straight (adjective)
with no bends or curls *a straight
road ; She's got straight hair.*

straight on (adverb)
without changing direction
*Turn right and then go straight on
for 1 kilometre.*

strange (adjective)
not normal *We heard a strange
noise upstairs.*

street (noun)
a road in a town with buildings on
each side *At night, the streets are
very quiet.*

strong (adjective)
A strong person
or thing has a
lot of power.
*a strong
man ; a
strong wind*

student (noun)
a person who is learning about a
subject *There are 30 students in
my English class.*

study (verb): **studies,
studying, studied**
to learn about a
subject *My sister is
studying history
at college.*

subject (noun)
something that you learn about *My favourite subject at school is maths.*

suddenly (adverb)
in a very quick way that surprises you *The car in front of us stopped suddenly.*

sugar (noun)
the white or brown grains that you put into food to make it taste sweet *Do you take sugar in your tea?*

suitcase (noun)
a large strong bag with flat sides that you put your clothes in when you travel

summer (noun)
the time of year between spring and autumn, when it is often hot *We go to the beach in the summer.*

sun (noun)
the big yellow ball in the sky that gives us heat and light *It's dangerous to look at the sun.*

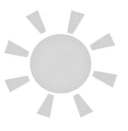

sunglasses (plural noun)
dark glasses that protect your eyes from the sun

sunny (adjective)
with a lot of bright sunshine *It's a lovely sunny day.*

supermarket (noun)
a large shop where you can buy food and things for the house

supper (noun)
a meal that you eat in the evening

sure (adjective)
You are sure when you know that something is true. *Are you sure you locked the door?*

surname (noun)
the name that you share with other people in your family *"Can you spell your surname?" "Yes, it's S-M-I-T-H."*

surprised (adjective)
You feel surprised when something happens that you weren't expecting.

swan (noun)
a large white bird with a long neck that lives on water

sweater (noun)
a warm piece of clothing that you wear on the top part of your body

a
b
c
d
e
f
g
h
i
j
k
l
m
n
o
p
q
r
s
t
u
v
w
x
y
z

a
b
c
d
e
f
g
h
i
j
k
l
m
n
o
p
q
r
s
t
u
v
w
x
y
z

sweet (adjective)
Sweet food tastes like sugar.
a cup of sweet tea

sweet (noun)
a small piece of sweet food such as a chocolate *Don't eat too many sweets!*

swim (verb):
swims, swimming, swam, swum
to move along in water using your arms and legs
Can you swim?

swimming pool (noun)
a large container filled with water for swimming

sword (noun)
a weapon with a short handle and a long sharp blade

Tt

T-shirt (noun)
a piece of clothing with short sleeves that you wear on the top part of your body

table (noun)
a piece of furniture with legs and a flat top *Come to the table – dinner's ready!*

table tennis (noun)
a sport in which two players stand either side of a table and hit a small white ball across a low net
a game of table tennis

tail (noun)
the long thin part at the back of an animal's body

take (verb): **takes, taking, took, taken**
1. to reach out and get something *Maria took another chocolate.*
2. to need a particular amount of time *The journey to Grandma's house takes three hours.*

3. You take a bus or train when you travel on it.
We always take the bus to school.
4. You take a photo when you use a camera or mobile phone to get a picture.

take off (verb): **takes off, taking off, took off, taken off** to remove clothes *Take off your shoes, please.*

talk (verb): **talks, talking, talked** to speak or have a conversation *The children listen when the teacher is talking. ; We talked for three hours.*

tall (adjective)
A tall person is not short. A tall building is high.
Amy is very tall. ; There are a lot of tall buildings in this part of the city.

taste (verb):
tastes, tasting, tasted
Something that tastes nice has a good flavour. *These strawberries taste lovely!*

taxi (noun)
a car with a driver that takes you to a place *We took a taxi to the airport.*

tea (noun)
1. a drink that you make by pouring hot water on to the leaves of the tea plant
a cup of tea
2. a small meal that you eat in the afternoon or early evening
We had sandwiches and a piece of cake for tea.

teach (verb): **teaches, teaching, taught** to tell people about a subject and help them to learn *Mrs Brown teaches English at our school.*

teacher (noun)
a person who teaches *I want to be a teacher when I grow up.*

team (noun)
a group of people who play a sport together *Jack is in the school football team.*

telephone (noun)
a device that you use to speak to someone who is in another place
The telephone rang and Diana answered it.

a b c d e f g h i j k l m n o p q r s **t** u v w x y z

television (noun)
a device with a screen for watching shows and films
We all sat in the living room and watched a film on television.

tell (verb): **tells, telling, told**
to say something to someone
Please tell me the answer!

temperature (noun)
how hot or cold a place, person or thing is *What's the temperature outside today? ; Keep the food at a low temperature.*

tennis (noun)
a sport in which two people stand at either end of a large area and hit a ball across a net *a tennis match*

tent (noun)
a shelter made of strong cloth for sleeping outside
We slept in a tent in the garden.

terrible (adjective)
very bad *The weather was terrible.*

test (noun)
a set of questions that you have to answer to show how much you know
We've got a maths test next week.

text (noun)
1. a written message that you send or receive using a mobile phone
send a text
2. a short piece of writing
Read the text and answer the questions.

text (verb): **texts, texting, texted**
to send someone a written message using a mobile phone *I texted you. Didn't you get it?*

thank (verb): **thanks, thanking, thanked** to say thank you to someone *Don't forget to thank Granny for the present!*

thank you (exclamation)
You say thank you to tell someone that you are happy that they did something for you. *"Thank you for your help." "You're welcome!"*

thanks (exclamation)
another word for "thank you", used with friends and family *"Thanks for that." "No problem!"*

theatre (noun)
a place where you go to see a play or a show

thick (adjective)
Thick clothes are heavy and warm.
I wear thick socks inside my boots.

thin (adjective)
A thin person does not have much fat on their body.

thing (noun)
an object *What's that thing on your desk?*

think (verb): **thinks, thinking, thought**
1. to have thoughts and ideas *"What are you doing?" "I'm thinking."*
2. to have an opinion *I think our new teacher is really nice.*

thirsty (adjective)
to need a drink *I'm very thirsty, Can I have some water, please?*

thousand (noun)
the number 1,000 *The car cost five thousand pounds.*

through (preposition)
from one side of something to the other *The train went through a tunnel.*

throw (verb): **throws, throwing, threw, thrown**
to use your strength to make something move through the air *Throw the ball to me!*

tick (noun)
a mark that a teacher puts on your work to show that an answer is correct

ticket (noun)
a small piece of paper or card that allows you to travel on a bus or a train *A return ticket to London, please.*

tidy (adjective)
A tidy room has everything in its proper place.

tie (noun)
a long piece of cloth that a man wears around his neck with a shirt

tie (verb): **ties, tying, tied**
to join two things together using string or a ribbon *She tied her hair up with a ribbon.*

tiger (noun)
a large wild animal that has yellow-orange fur with black stripes

tights (plural noun)
a piece of clothing that covers the feet and the legs up to the waist *a pair of tights*

a
b
c
d
e
f
g
h
i
j
k
l
m
n
o
p
q
r
s
t
u
v
w
x
y
z

a
b
c
d
e
f
g
h
i
j
k
l
m
n
o
p
q
r
s
t
u
v
w
x
y
z

time (noun)
1. the number of minutes or hours that you spend doing something
I spend a lot of time doing homework.
2. the hour and the minute at any point during the day *"What time is it?" "Ten o'clock."*

timetable (noun)
a list that shows when things will happen during the day *What time is our English lesson? I've lost my timetable!*

tired (adjective)
You are tired when you feel that you want to have a rest or you need to sleep.
We're all tired after our long journey.

today (adverb)
on this day *I'm busy today but I'm not doing anything tomorrow.*

toe (noun)
one of the five separate parts at the end of your foot

together (adverb)
People are together when they are with each other or in a group.
Jack and Hannah are always together.

toilet (noun)
a seat over a hole where you go to get rid of waste from your body
I need to go to the toilet. ; Where are the toilets, please?

tomato (noun): **tomatoes**
a soft round red fruit that people eat in salads or sauces
spaghetti with tomato sauce

tomorrow (adverb)
on the day after today
Bye, see you tomorrow!

tonight (adverb)
in the evening or during the night of today *I'm going to the cinema with Kirsty tonight.*

too (adverb)
also *Can I come too?*

tooth (noun): **teeth**
one of the hard white parts in your mouth that you use when you eat *My tooth hurts. I need to go to the dentist.*

toothbrush (noun): **toothbrushes**
a small brush that you use to clean your teeth

top (noun)
1. the highest part of something *the top of the mountain*
2. a piece of clothing that you wear on the upper part of your body *a stripy top*

torch (noun): **torches**
a small electric light that you can carry

towel (noun)
a large piece of thick material that you use to dry yourself after washing or swimming *a beach towel*

tower (noun)
a tall narrow part of a building *The lonely princess lived in a tower.*

town (noun)
a place with streets and buildings, where a lot of people live and work *I live in a small town not far from Manchester.*

toy (noun)
something that children play with *There were toys all over the floor in Mary's bedroom.*

traffic (noun)
all the cars, lorries, etc., that move on roads *There's always a lot of traffic in town.*

train (noun)
a vehicle with several parts that are joined together and pulled along a railway by an engine *I'm getting the 10 o'clock train to London.*

travel (verb): **travels, travelling, travelled** to go on a journey or visit several places *We spent the summer travelling around Europe.*

treasure (noun)
in stories, a collection of valuable things like jewellery or gold that someone finds *a treasure chest*

a
b
c
d
e
f
g
h
i
j
k
l
m
n
o
p
q
r
s
t
u
v
w
x
y
z

a
b
c
d
e
f
g
h
i
j
k
l
m
n
o
p
q
r
s
t
u
v
w
x
y
z

tree (noun)
a tall plant with a wooden trunk and branches
an apple tree

trip (noun)
a short journey to a place and back again *a trip to the zoo*

trousers (plural noun)
a piece of clothing that you wear on your legs
These trousers are too long for me!

truck (noun)
the American word for "lorry"
a truck driver

try (verb): **tries, trying, tried**
1. to do your best to make something happen
Try harder. You can do it!
2. to see if you like something
Try this sauce. I think you'll like it.

turn (verb): **turns, turning, turned**
to move so that you are facing in a different direction *Turn around so I can see you. ; Turn left after the post office.*

turn off (verb): **turns off, turning off, turned off** to stop electricity, gas or water from flowing to something *Turn off the lights when you leave the room, please.*

turn on (verb): **turns on, turning on, turned on** to make electricity, gas or water flow to something
She turned on the tap and filled the glass with water.

TV (noun)
another word for television
Shall we stay at home and watch TV?

twice (adverb)
two times *I've been to London twice.*

Uu

ugly (adjective)
not pretty or beautiful
an ugly building

umbrella (noun)
an object that you
hold over your head
when it is raining

uncle (noun)
the brother of your mother or father,
or your aunt's husband
a photo of my uncle and my cousin

under (preposition)
in a place that is lower than
something else *Kate was hiding
under the table.*

understand (verb): **understands,
understanding, understood**
to know what something means
*I don't understand. Could you repeat
that, please?*

uniform (noun)
the special clothes that you wear to
show that you are part of a group,
or that you go to a particular school
school uniform

untidy (adjective)
An untidy room is not organized
and has a lot of things in the wrong
place. *Michael's bedroom is always
untidy, with toys all over the floor.*

until (preposition)
Something happens until a
particular time when it continues
up to that time and stops. *I waited
until 9:30 but no one came so I left.*

unusual (adjective)
strange or different *There are some
unusual plants in the garden.*

upstairs (adverb)
from a lower to a higher floor in
a building *William went upstairs
to bed.*

use (verb): **uses, using, used**
to do a job with something
Would you like to use my pen?

used to (phrase)
If you used to do something, you did
it in the past. *I used to watch TV
every night, but I don't now.*

usually (adverb)
most of the time; very often *Tania
usually goes to bed at 9 o'clock.*

a
b
c
d
e
f
g
h
i
j
k
l
m
n
o
p
q
r
s
t
u
v
w
x
y
z

Vv

valley (noun)
an area of low land between hills

vegetable (noun)
a plant that
you can eat,
such as a
carrot or an onion

*It's important to eat
lots of fresh vegetables.*

very (adverb)
You use "very" to make an adjective
stronger. *It's very hot outside today.*

video (noun)
a recording of moving pictures
and sound

video (verb): **videos, videoing,
videoed** to record a video
Dad videoed us dancing.

view (noun)
all the things you can see from
a place *We had a beautiful view
of the mountains from our
hotel room.*

village (noun)
a very small town *Priya grew up
in a small village in India.*

violin (noun)
a musical instrument
with four strings. You
hold it under your
chin and play it
using a long thin
object called a bow.
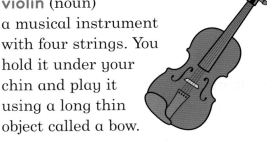

visit (verb): **visits, visiting, visited**
to go to someone's house and spend
some time with them *We visit
Granny and Grandad every Sunday.*

voice (noun)
the sound that comes from your
mouth when you speak or sing
*Sara has a very quiet voice. ;
The boys in the choir have
beautiful voices.*

volleyball (noun)
a sport in which two teams use their
hands and arms to hit a ball over a
high net *a volleyball match*

a
b
c
d
e
f
g
h
i
j
k
l
m
n
o
p
q
r
s
t
u

v
w
x
y
z

Ww

wait (verb): **waits, waiting, waited**
to stay where you are until something happens or someone comes *We waited for the bus to arrive.*

waiter (noun)
someone whose job is to serve people in a restaurant *The waiter came and took our order.*

wake up (verb): **wakes up, waking up, woke up, woken up**
to stop sleeping and open your eyes *I woke up early and went downstairs.*

walk (verb): **walks, walking, walked** to move along putting one foot in front of the other *I walk to school every morning.*

walk (noun)
a short journey that you make by walking *Shall we go for a walk?*

wall (noun)
a structure made of stone or brick around a park or a garden *She climbed over the garden wall.*

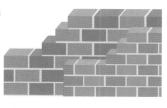

wand (noun)
a thin stick used for doing magic *a magic wand*

want (verb): **wants, wanting, wanted** to feel you would like to have or do something *I want a dog.*

war (noun)
There is a war when two or more countries fight against each other. *The two countries are at war.*

warm (adjective)
fairly hot in a nice way *The sun felt lovely and warm on my face.*

wash (noun): **washes**
You have a wash when you wash your body.

wash (verb): **washes, washing, washed** to make something clean with soap and water *Wash your hands.*

a
b
c
d
e
f
g
h
i
j
k
l
m
n
o
p
q
r
s
t
u
v
w
x
y
z

watch (noun): **watches**
a small clock that you
wear on your wrist

watch (verb):
watches, watching, watched
to look at someone doing something
We watched the girls playing football.

water (noun)
the liquid that is in rivers, lakes and
the sea *a glass of water*

watermelon (noun)
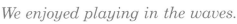
a large round green
fruit with pink
flesh inside

wave (noun)
one of the
lines of
water that
rise up on the
surface of the sea
We enjoyed playing in the waves.

wave (verb): **waves, waving,
waved** to raise your hand and
move it from side to side to say
hello or goodbye *We waved as the
car drove away.*

way (noun)
the route you take to go somewhere
*Can you tell me the way to the
swimming pool?*

weak (adjective)
A weak person does not have much
power or strength. *Grandad is still
weak after his illness.*

wear (verb): **wears, wearing,
wore, worn** to have clothes on your
body *I'm wearing my new jeans.*

weather (noun)
how hot or cold it is and the rain,
sunshine or wind in a particular
area *What's the weather like outside?*

website (noun)
a place on the internet where
you can read information about
something

week (noun)
a period of seven days *We're going
on holiday for two weeks.*

weekend (noun)
Saturday and Sunday, when many
people don't go to school or work
What are you doing at the weekend?

welcome (exclamation)
something you say to people to show
that you are glad they have come
Welcome to our school!

well (adjective)
healthy and not ill
I'm not feeling very well.

well (adverb)
in a good or satisfactory way
Louise sings well.

well done (exclamation)
something you say to someone
who has done a good piece of work
*You've worked really hard –
well done!*

west (noun)

the direction on the left
of a map *He lives in a
small town in the west
of England.*

wet (adjective)
not dry; covered with water *We put
our wet clothes in the dryer.*

whale (noun)
a very large animal
that lives in
the sea

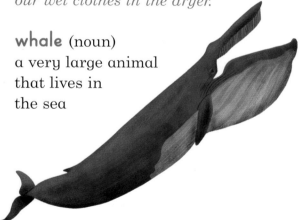

wheel (noun)
one of the round objects on a bicycle,
car, bus, etc., that turn and make it
move along *a bicycle wheel*

whisper (verb): **whispers,
whispering, whispered**
to speak very quietly
"Shhh!" she whispered.

whistle (verb): **whistles, whistling,
whistled** to make a high loud sound
by blowing air through your lips

white (adjective)
the colour of snow *The fields were
white with snow.*

why (adverb)
a word you use to ask the reason for
something *Why is the sky blue?*

wide (adjective)
a large distance from one side to
the other *a wide road*

wife (noun): **wives**
a woman that someone is married to
This is my wife, Anya.

wild (adjective)
Wild animals live in the countryside
or the jungle without help from
humans.

will (verb)
1. You use "will" with another verb
to talk about the future.
When will we arrive?
2. You use "will" with another verb
to offer to do something for someone.
I will carry those bags for you.

a
b
c
d
e
f
g
h
i
j
k
l
m
n
o
p
q
r
s
t
u
v
w
x
y
z

a
b
c
d
e
f
g
h
i
j
k
l
m
n
o
p
q
r
s
t
u
v
w
x
y
z

win (verb): **wins, winning, won**
You win a competition or a race when you come first, before all the other people. *Elsa won the writing competition. ; Who won the race?*

wind (noun)
the air that moves around you so that you can feel it *A warm wind blew from the west.*

window (noun)
a glass opening in the wall of a building *Can I open the window?*

windy (adjective)
It is windy if a strong wind is blowing.
a windy day

wing (noun)
the parts of a bird's or insect's body that it uses to fly
a butterfly's colourful wings

winner (noun)
the person who comes first in a race or competition *The winner of the competition gets a prize.*

winter (noun)
the time of year between autumn and spring, when it is usually cold
In winter, we wear warm clothes.

wish (verb): **wishes, wishing, wished** to want something very much *I wish I was rich!*

without (preposition)
used for talking about something that you do not have or do not do *I did my homework without any help.*

wizard (noun)
in stories, a man who has magic powers

wolf (noun): **wolves**
a wild animal like a large dog

woman (noun): **women**
an adult female person
an old woman

wonderful (adjective)
extremely good *We had a wonderful holiday in Italy.*

wood (noun)
1. the hard material that trees are made of *The children collected wood for the fire.*
2. an area of land where there are a lot of trees *The little house was in the middle of a dark wood.*

wool (noun)
the thick hair that grows on sheep, used for making warm clothes

word (noun)
a group of letters with a meaning *What does this word mean?*

work (noun)
a job or task that you have to do *You've done a lot of work today – well done!*

work (verb): **works, working, worked** to do a job or task *Mum works for a company in the city. ; You have to work hard at school.*

world (noun)
the planet that we live on *What is the biggest city in the world?*

worried (adjective)
You are worried if you are unhappy because you think something bad will happen. *Harry had a worried look on his face.*

worry (verb): **worries, worrying, worried** to feel unhappy because you think something bad will happen *Don't worry – everything will be all right!*

worse (adjective)
more unpleasant or bad than something else *Your handwriting is worse than mine!*

worst (adjective)
more unpleasant or bad than all other things *That's the worst film I've ever seen!*

would like (phrase)
used for politely saying what you want *I would like three chocolate ice creams, please.*

write (verb): **writes, writing, wrote, written** to use a pen to put words on a page *Please write your name on your homework.*

wrong (adjective)
not correct *We took the wrong bus and missed the film.*

a
b
c
d
e
f
g
h
i
j
k
l
m
n
o
p
q
r
s
t
u
v
w
x
y
z

a
b
c
d
e
f
g
h
i
j
k
l
m
n
o
p
q
r
s
t
u
v
w
x
y
z

Xx

X-ray (noun)
a photograph of the bones and other parts inside your body

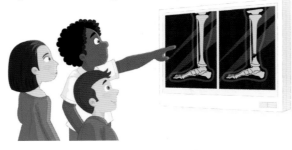

xylophone (noun)
a musical instrument that you play with sticks that have soft balls on the end

Yy

year (noun)
a period of 365 days or twelve months *I lived in Chicago for one year.*

yellow (adjective)
the colour of the sun or the middle of an egg *We painted the walls yellow.*

yesterday (adverb)
the day before today
Sara was ill yesterday but she's much better today.

yet (adverb)
until now *Have you done your homework yet?*

you (pronoun)
not me, but the other person

you're welcome (phrase)
used to reply to someone who has said thank you *"Thank you." "You're welcome."*

young (adjective)
A young person
is not old.
*The young
children
went to bed
at 7.30 p.m.*

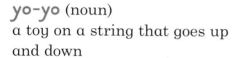

yo-yo (noun)
a toy on a string that goes up
and down

Zz

zebra (noun)
an animal with
black and
white stripes

zero (noun)
the number 0 *Four minus four
equals zero (4 − 4 = 0).*

zip (noun)
a type of fastening especially
for trousers and jackets

zoo (noun)
a public place where you can
go and look at animals such as
lions, giraffes and monkeys *a trip
to the zoo*

a
b
c
d
e
f
g
h
i
j
k
l
m
n
o
p
q
r
s
t
u
v
w
x
y
z

Noun

A noun is a naming word.
You can tell a noun by whether you can put the word "the" or "a" in front of it. Some nouns are things you can touch:

tree	school
glove	door

Some are things you cannot touch:

week	trouble
sound	language

Proper noun

A proper noun is the name of a person or place. It begins with a capital letter:

Anna	Tony
London	Australia

Adjective

An adjective describes a noun:

big	soft
scary	happy
pretty	tall
old	shiny

Verb

A verb is a doing word or a being word:

act	drink
look	talk
jump	write
swim	read

Most verbs have these endings:

walk	walks	walking	walked
dance	dances	dancing	danced

Some verbs have different endings:

be	is	being	was
buy	buys	buying	bought
carry	carries	carrying	carried
come	comes	coming	came
do	does	doing	did
get	gets	getting	got
give	gives	giving	gave
go	goes	going	went
have	has	having	had
run	runs	running	ran
say	says	saying	said
see	sees	seeing	saw
sit	sits	sitting	sat
take	takes	taking	took

Adverb

An adverb describes a verb.
Many adverbs end in "-ly":

quickly   **nicely**
smoothly   **tightly**

But some adverbs do not end in "-ly":

soon   **enough**
fast   **again**

Prepositions

These describe positions or directions:

at   by   for   with   between
in   on   to   underneath

Question words

Use these words to ask a question:

Who?   **When?**
Where?   **Which?**
What?   **How?**
Why?   **Whose?**

Connective words

These words are sometimes called conjunctions. Use them to join two sentences together:

and   **but**
because   **so**

some adjectives

thin

fat

muddy

spotty

white

brown

some adverbs

He ran home **quickly**.

I shouted **loudly**.

She played the piano **beautifully**.

Numbers

Cardinal numbers

1	one	11	eleven	30	thirty
2	two	12	twelve	40	forty
3	three	13	thirteen	50	fifty
4	four	14	fourteen	60	sixty
5	five	15	fifteen	70	seventy
6	six	16	sixteen	80	eighty
7	seven	17	seventeen	90	ninety
8	eight	18	eighteen	100	one hundred
9	nine	19	nineteen	1,000	one thousand
10	ten	20	twenty	1,000,000	one million

Ordinal numbers

1st	first	9th	ninth
2nd	second	10th	tenth
3rd	third	11th	eleventh
4th	fourth	12th	twelfth
5th	fifth	20th	twentieth
6th	sixth	100th	one hundredth
7th	seventh	1,000th	one thousandth
8th	eighth	1,000,000th	one millionth

Measurements

Length

mm	millimetres	10mm	= 1cm
cm	centimetres	100cm	= 1m
m	metres	1,000m	= 1km
km	kilometres		

Weight

mg	milligrams	1,000mg	= 1g
g	grams	1,000g	= 1kg
kg	kilograms		

Capacity

ml	millilitres	10ml	= 1cl
cl	centilitres	100cl	= 1l
l	litres		

O'clock

When the big minute hand points straight up at the 12, we say the time is **o'clock**. This clock is showing 10 o'clock.

10:00

7:00

8:00

12:00

4:00

Half past

When the big minute hand is halfway round the clock and points at the 6, we say the time is **half past**. This clock is showing half past 4.

4:30

Quarter past

When the big minute hand points to the 3, we say it is **quarter past**. This clock shows quarter past 4.

4:15

Quarter to

When the big minute hand points to the 9, we say it is **quarter to**. This clock shows quarter to 5.

4:45

Shapes

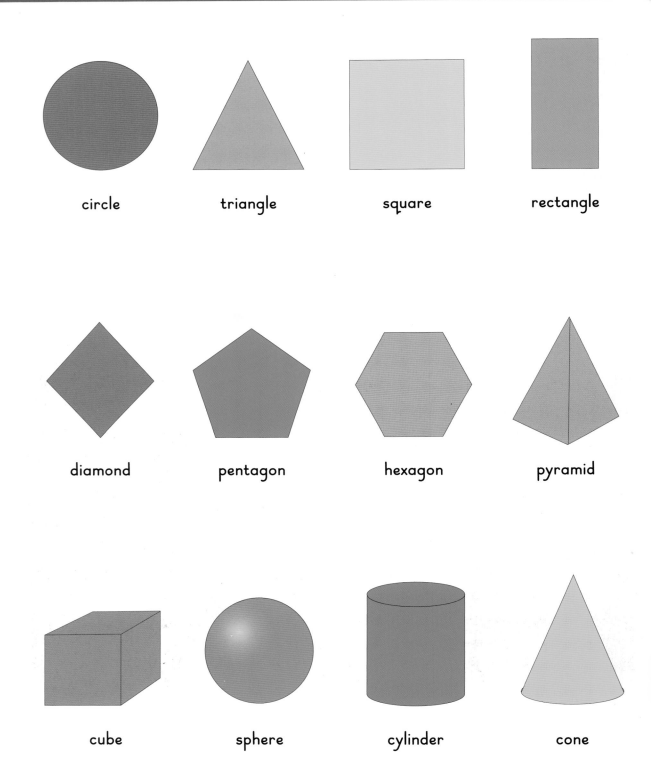

circle

triangle

square

rectangle

diamond

pentagon

hexagon

pyramid

cube

sphere

cylinder

cone

red

yellow

blue

green

orange

purple

pink

brown

grey

black

white

Fruit

apple

banana

blueberries

kiwi fruit

lemon

melon

orange

peach

pear

pineapple

plum

raspberry

strawberry

tomato

aubergine   bean   broccoli   cabbage

 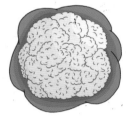 

carrot   cauliflower   cucumber   leek

lettuce   onion   pea   potato

sweetcorn   turnip

cat

chick

cockerel

cow

dog

fish

goat

goose

guinea pig

hamster

hen

horse

kitten

mouse

pig

puppy

rabbit

sheep

tortoise

bear

crocodile

dolphin

elephant

giraffe

kangaroo

lion

monkey

penguin

polar bear

seal

shark

tiger

whale

zebra

Vehicles

aeroplane

ambulance

bicycle

boat

bus

car

fire engine

lorry

motorbike

tractor

train

van

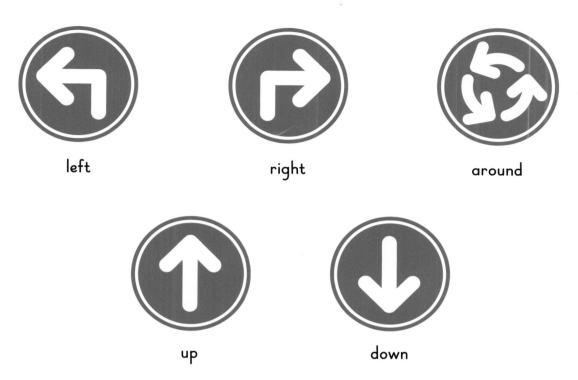

left

right

around

up

down

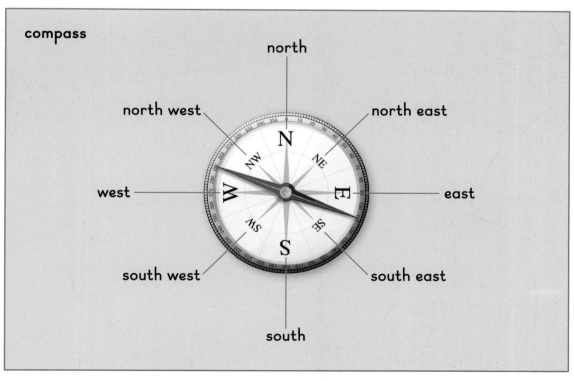

compass

north

north west

north east

west

east

south west

south east

south

Days of the week

There are seven days in the week.

Monday
Tuesday
Wednesday
Thursday
Friday
Saturday
Sunday

Months of the year

There are twelve months in the year.

January
February
March
April
May
June
July
August
September
October
November
December

To help you remember . . .
Thirty days has September,
April, June and November;
All the rest have thirty-one,
Except for February alone.
And that has twenty-eight days clear,
And twenty-nine in each leap year.

grandmother / grandma

mum / mother

brother

grandfather / grandpa

dad / father

sister

Other family members
aunt
uncle
niece
nephew
cousin

What is the weather?

The weather is all around us, all of the time. It can change from hot to cold, wet to dry, or calm to windy, or it can stay the same for days.

The sun

It gives out light and heat. The heat warms the ground and then the air. This makes the air move.

Clouds

These are made of millions of tiny floating drops of water.

Wind

This is made by warm and cold air moving about. It moves the clouds and brings changes in the weather.

Rain

This happens when tiny drops of water in a cloud join to make large drops, that then fall from the sky.

Storms

These have fast winds and lots of rain. Thunderstorms have flashes of lightning, and loud booms of thunder.

What are the seasons?

The weather changes through the year. These changes are called the seasons.

Winter

Days are usually cold and cloudy, and there is often rain. In very cold weather, the raindrops freeze and fall as snow.

Spring

Days become warmer, with more daylight hours. There are fewer clouds and less rain. Plants start to grow and flowers come out.

Summer

Days are warm or hot, with more bright sunshine. There is little wind and there might be no rain for weeks.

Autumn

Days are cooler, with more rain and fewer daylight hours. There may be storms, and the leaves fall from the trees.

At home

Can you match the objects below to the rooms they are found in?

 toaster

 knife

 fork

 toys

 television

 toilet

 duck

 lamp

 wardrobe

 brush

 jug

 sofa

 iron

 shower

 cushion

 mirror

 kettle

bowl

living room

kitchen

dining room

bedroom

bathroom

At school

The children are busy playing and learning.

What is your favourite thing to do at school?

Look at all the objects below. Where are they in the big picture?

computer

chair

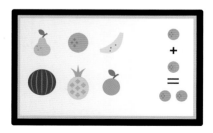

whiteboard

blocks

brush

tablet

scissors

mouse

drum

stickers

painting

book

The body

Inside

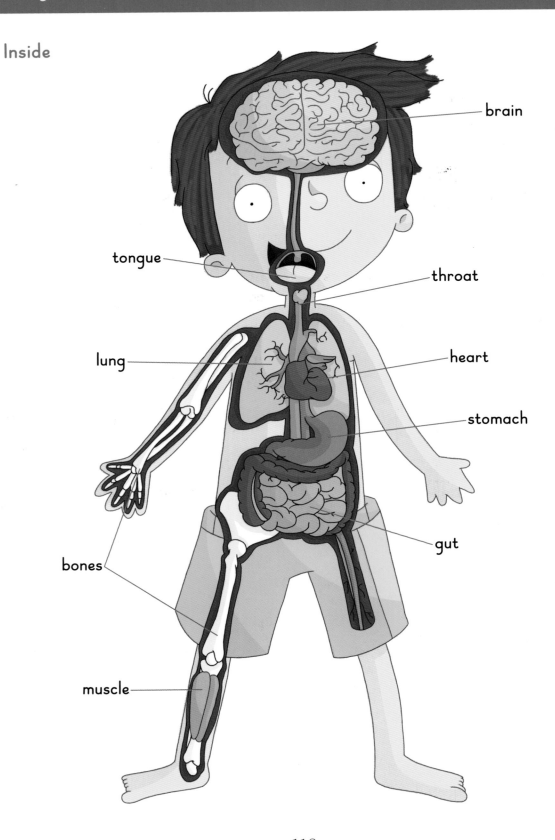

brain

tongue

throat

lung

heart

stomach

gut

bones

muscle

Outside

head

hair

face

eye

mouth

nose

ear

chin

jaw

neck

shoulder

arm

. chest.

tummy

elbow

back

thumb

hip

hand

finger

knee

leg

ankle

foot (feet)

heel

toe

a b c d e f g h i j k l m n o p q r s t u v w x y z

Now you have seen the full alphabet from A–Z, why not try some word activities of your own?

Collect new words

In your notebook, write down any new words you hear or see, and then write down what you think they mean. At the end of the week, look for the words in your dictionary and check to see if you were right.

Draw a picture of a noun

Find a noun in the dictionary and cover the meaning, then draw a picture of the word in a notebook. You can then check the word's description against your drawing to see if you were right.

Word-search game

Try to play this speed word-search game with your friends. One person looks for a word in their dictionary and then calls out the word. The other players then have to find the word as quickly as they can. The person who finds the word first is the winner!

Label things in your house

Walk around your house and see if you can write down the word for the things you see on a piece of paper.